"This book is truly magnificent. These are answers ~~...~~ ~~...~~ ..d proven to work. They are the best available to Christian parents, friends and spouses. God's guidance and truth are present on every page."
Willa Medinger, Regeneration Books

"Worthen and Davies's book faces the reality that can no longer be hidden—homosexuality and AIDS are devastating many of today's Christian families. The helpful, healing and sound text covers the tumultuous emotions family members grapple with."
John White

"When people put down their misconceptions and pick up this book, they will find truth that will lead them to hope."
Stephen Arterburn

"This book is filled with biblically grounded guidance seasoned by years of ministry 'in the trenches' with gay persons and their loved ones. It is written at a practical and understandable level and presents an array of realistic stories from real life."
Stan Jones, author of *The Gay Debate*

"This practical, easy-to-read narrative is full of sound advice for anyone who has a homosexual loved one. It makes good psychological sense and reflects the wisdom of the writers' life experiences."
Joseph Nicolosi, author of *Reparative Therapy of Male Homosexuality*

"*Someone I Love Is Gay* is practical, compassionate and long overdue. Worthen and Davies have combined their unique insights on one of the most vexing issues facing Christian families today . . . and have written an invaluable guide for anyone wanting to know how to respond to a homosexual friend or relative."
Joe Dallas, author of *Desires in Conflict*

"This book is a must resource for any parent reeling from the news that a son or daughter is gay."
Mike Yorkey, *Focus on the Family* magazine editor

"Few people are as knowledgeable about the volatile subject of homosexuality as Bob Davies. What he writes on the subject, I read, because he is credible and compassionate and speaks the truth in love."
Cal Thomas

"*Someone I Love Is Gay* speaks to the heart of parents who have come to know that their son or daughter . . . has declared himself/herself 'gay.' . . . This volume will help all those who counsel such parents to counsel still better."
Rev. John F. Harvey, O.S.F.S., director of Courage

"This book will be really helpful, especially to parents. It will also be a great tool for pastors and leaders. The information is fabulous."
Barbara Johnson

SOMEONE I LOVE IS GAY

HOW FAMILY & FRIENDS CAN RESPOND

Anita Worthen & Bob Davies

InterVarsity Press
Downers Grove, Illinois

InterVarsity Press® is the book-publishing division of InterVarsity Christian Fellowship®, a student movement active on campus at hundreds of universities, colleges and schools of nursing in the United States of America, and a member movement of the International Fellowship of Evangelical Students. For information about local and regional activities, write Public Relations Dept., InterVarsity Christian Fellowship, 6400 Schroeder Rd., P.O. Box 7895, Madison, WI 53707-7895.

All Scripture quotations, unless otherwise indicated, are taken from the HOLY BIBLE, NEW INTERNATIONAL VERSION®. NIV®. Copyright © 1973, 1978, 1984 by International Bible Society. Used by permission of Zondervan Publishing House. All rights reserved.

Cover background: Roberta Polfus
ISBN 0-8308-1982-7

Printed in the United States of America ♾

Library of Congress Cataloging-in-Publication Data

Worthen, Anita, 1944-
   Someone I love is gay: how family and friends can respond/Anita
Worthen and Bob Davies.
     p.   cm.
   Includes bibliographical references.
   ISBN 0-8308-1982-7 (paper: alk. paper)
   1. Homosexuality—Religious aspects—Christianity—Controversial
literature. 2. Church work with gays. I. Davies, Bob, 1951-
II. Title.
BR115.H6W67   1996
261.8'35766—dc20   96-11252
                                        CIP

| 17 | 16 | 15 | 14 | 13 | 12 | 11 | 10 | 9 | 8 | 7 | 6 | | | |
| 10 | 09 | 08 | 07 | 06 | 05 | 04 | 03 | 02 | 01 | 00 | 99 | 98 |

To Barbara Johnson,
who for more than twenty years
has ministered comfort to untold thousands
throughout the world.
You are a faithful friend
and a steadfast coworker in a needy harvest field.
We love you.

Acknowledgments

We give sincerest thanks to the whole team who made this book possible: to our friends worldwide who prayed and cheered us on; to Becky Cain, for transcribing hours of taped interviews with her usual cheerful enthusiasm; to Frank Worthen, for his extensive editing of Anita's rough drafts; to Pam Davies, for her unswerving support in so many ways; to Cindy Bunch-Hotaling, our skilled and encouraging editor at InterVarsity Press; to our critique team who gave helpful feedback on the first draft, including Nancy Anderson, Wendell Anderson, Sandra Aslesen, Beth Babb, Georgia Beaverson, Ed Blake, Kathleen Bremner, Barbara Driskill, Michael Driskill, Bob Fisher, Kathy Fisher, Doug Hansen, Wanda Harris, Doug Houck, Jeanne Ann Jackson, Barbara Johnson, Mildred Kelley, Chris MacKenzie, Willa Medinger, Kevin Oshiro, John Paulk, Lori Rentzel, Mona Riley, DebbieLynne Simmons, Gloria Swihart, Anne Taylor, Tom Taylor; to all the family members and friends who shared the deepest parts of their hearts with us in the hope that others might benefit from their experience.

And we thank the Lord for putting us together as a writing team. We thank him for the inspiration to pursue this project and the strength to accomplish the writing in record time. If lives are changed by this book, he is the one who will accomplish it.

Introduction: How This Book Can Help You

For many years we, the authors, have been aware of the need for a book like this, one that offers help to people grappling with the homosexuality of a person close to them. If you are in crisis over the homosexuality of someone you care deeply about, this book is for you. Even if you are past the "crisis" stage but the hurt remains, we believe these pages will help you.

We wrote this book especially for parents, spouses and friends. But other family members, as well as pastors and counselors who minister to families facing this crisis, will find the book helpful.

We suggest that, no matter what your relationship is to someone dealing with homosexuality or lesbianism, you begin with chapter one and read through the first seven chapters. Then, since chapters eight through eleven deal with particular situations, you can turn to the ones appropriate for you: chapter eight is for parents, chapter nine is for spouses, chapter ten is for friends and chapter eleven is for those dating or engaged to someone struggling with same-sex attractions. The final chapter applies to all readers.

One of the authors, Anita Worthen, has a son currently practicing homosexuality. After raising Tony by herself as a single mother, she married Frank Worthen in 1984. Since then, Anita and Frank (a former homosexual) have ministered to Christians struggling with homosexual and lesbian issues and to their friends and families. For six years Anita worked at Love In Action, the ex-gay ministry that Frank had founded in 1973. Then, in response to Frank's vision for overseas ministry, they resigned from Love In Action and traveled to the Philippines, where they established an outreach to homosexuals in Manila. In late 1994, after turning the Manila ministry over to Filipino leaders, they returned to their home city of San Rafael, California, and established another ex-gay ministry, New Hope, where they have worked together since then.

Anita is the primary "voice" of the book. All mentions of "I" and "me" throughout the book refer to her.

Coauthor Bob Davies is a middle-aged man who grew up attending church. Yet from the age of twelve he realized that he was sexually attracted to other men. At college he discovered the large gay scene in his home city of Vancouver, Canada. He felt drawn to it, but out of fear and timidity he stayed away from the gay bars and other meeting places for homosexual men.

Several years later, Bob renewed his commitment to Christ and left Vancouver to attend Bible college, where a firm foundation was laid for his future life and ministry. After graduation and several years' involvement in short-term missions, he discovered the existence of ex-gay ministries and moved to California to find specialized help for his lingering homosexual feelings. Soon he became involved in full-time ministry to other men and women struggling with homosexual issues and eventually was appointed executive director of Exodus International—North America, a coalition of ex-gay ministries. He has been happily married since 1985.

So Bob writes from the perspective of someone who has struggled with homosexuality in his own life, plus he draws from years of experience in counseling hundreds of family members and friends with a gay loved one.

The stories in this book are based on the lives of real people. In cases where first names only are used, names and identifying details have been altered to protect the privacy of the individuals involved.

We hope this book will give you insight, encouragement and strength as you deal with this perplexing situation. If we can provide even one small step forward in your journey toward understanding and healing, the months of hard work that went into this writing project will have been abundantly worthwhile.

Read Chapters 1-7

1

Homosexuality: The Shocking Discovery

W hen my sixteen-year-old son Tony began staying out all night, I (Anita) became very concerned. I didn't even know the names of most of his friends. One day I slipped into his bedroom to find out what was going on. I found a piece of paper in his wallet and began scribbling down the names and phone numbers. Suddenly Tony walked in.

"Whaddya think you're doing?" he yelled, his eyes blazing.

I could feel my face flush with embarrassment, but I kept my voice calm. "Tony, I want to know where you are. When you don't come home, I've got to know who to call."

We argued for several minutes, then he dropped the bombshell. "Well, you know I'm gay, don't you?"

My mind froze. Tony began filling the awkward silence with horrifying details. Three months before, he'd been hitchhiking home when a school guidance counselor had picked him up and seduced him. Now he accepted his "new" identity and was getting to know other homosexuals.

"Mom," he concluded, "I've found the man of my dreams. Everything's going to be all right now!"

In the days following I was haunted by every mistake I had ever made as a mother. I thought back to the beginning, when at age eighteen I'd eloped with my boyfriend. Somehow we never got around to making our marriage official. Soon afterward, I became pregnant, and I moved home with my parents. Everyone assumed that I had gotten divorced, so I hid the fact that I was actually an unwed expectant mother.

A few years later my brother became a Christian. One night I went with him to a Bible study and noticed something different in the people I met. I went home and started talking to God. "I've been doing it my way," I told him, "but now I'm willing to try your way."

In the following weeks I sensed a new power in my life to make right choices. I began attending a local church, and I prayed every night that God would be a husband to me and a father to my son. Soon I was working with other single mothers in my church, and others held me up as the perfect example of single parenthood.

But after several years I began feeling burned out. I would go to work, come home and sit in front of the TV; on Sunday mornings I'd drag myself to church. Then God allowed some difficult circumstances to enter my life, and I started drawing close to him again, praying and reading my Bible. Soon I felt a renewed closeness with God.

Homosexuality Hits Home

At the same time, I saw that my relationship with my son was not good. We had grown far apart. Tony, now a teenager, had acquired many new friends whom I didn't know. Soon afterward came his confession of homosexual involvement. "I don't understand this," I told Tony that day, "but I love you and we'll work it out."

My response was the only thing that I did right for the next two weeks. I had no knowledge at all of how to deal with this situation. But I knew one thing: I would do *anything* to stop that man from putting his arms around my son ever again. Then I came up with the perfect solution: we would kidnap Tony! I telephoned one of my brothers, who arranged to fly Tony to another brother's home in central Oregon. The next day when my son arrived home from school, we loaded all his things into a car and drove him to the airport. Before Tony knew what hit him, he was on his way to Oregon.

I thought the whole problem was solved. Tony's gay friends were in California, and now he was eleven hundred miles away in a little Oregon town. Perfect. My brother promised to look after him until I could join them.

I immediately gave my notice at work. They were probably relieved when I finally left two weeks later; I cried continually and walked around in a fog the whole time. The guilt feelings overwhelmed me, and I could turn to no one for encouragement. *This might never have happened if you had married,* I lectured myself, certain that no other Christian mother had found herself in my situation.

At this time in my life I hit my low point in terms of dealing with the reality of my son's homosexuality. I'll be sharing more of my story in coming chapters, and things *do* get better, I promise! If you are a parent, you probably have gone through many of the same feelings I described; you have felt the same pain, the same sense of panic, the same over-whelming guilt. The next chapters look at these emotions and suggest ways of dealing with them. We will also talk about many other issues that concern parents.

Troubled Marriages

Spouses of homosexuals face similar difficulties, but in addition they face a great threat to their marriages and therefore an intensified pain when confronted with the possible loss of their marriage partner. You may be able to relate to Beth Babb's story.[1]

In June 1985, Beth realized that she and her husband, Mike, had a serious problem in their ten-year marriage. But she couldn't figure out exactly what was wrong.

Beth and Mike were both committed Christians. Mike had always been a generous, fun-loving jokester. But lately he had turned into a brooding, unpredictable stranger. The changes in her husband frightened Beth.

Her close friend Julie had seen the same startling changes in Mike, and they talked about the situation for a long time.

Finally Julie told Beth, "I think I know what is wrong. When I pray about Mike, two words keep getting impressed on my heart." She glanced over at Beth. "One is *suicide*—and the other is *homosexuality.*" Deep inside Beth sensed that her friend was right, and she felt a searing pain.

Later, Julie talked privately with Mike over the phone. "I think I know what is troubling you."

Mike was skeptical. "Oh, really?"

Julie reminded Mike of her love, then said boldly, "You are struggling with homosexuality . . . and suicide."

Mike began crying.

Julie felt a mixture of sadness and relief as she heard Mike's reaction. The truth was finally out in the open.

"What are you going to do about it?" she probed.

"I don't know." Mike gave a heavy sigh. "I just don't know." Julie told him that no matter what, she still loved him.

After Julie hung up, Beth entered their bedroom, where Mike was sitting on the bed. "Don't you think it's time you told me?" she asked.

Mike looked up. "I'm gay," he said calmly, though the words ripped through Beth's heart like poisoned arrows. Her worst fears had come true.

An Open Wound

The next day Beth felt like an open, oozing wound. She wondered whether Mike would even return home from work, or if he would run off and desert her. She grieved over their three children: how would this crisis affect them?

Amid her turmoil, Beth knew that God was calling her to continue loving Mike. "Don't desert him," the Lord whispered to her heart. "My grace is sufficient for you." She sensed God's assurance that he would take care of Mike. But she knew they had a long, hard struggle ahead.

That evening, Beth and Mike went to their favorite restaurant for a private conversation away from the children. "What direction do you want to go?" she asked him.

Mike's deep brown eyes were sad. "I want my marriage, my family. I don't want homosexuality, but I can't make it on my own. I need a miracle from God."

Beth remembered what the Lord had shown her earlier in the day, and she told Mike that she'd never reject him. "I'm ready to stand with you. I'll support you in every way possible."

Their commitment to each other somehow carried them through the discouraging days that followed. "We were like children groping in the dark," Beth recalls. "We had no earthly resources; we only knew to hang on to Jesus. I had never heard of anyone being delivered from homosexuality. It seemed a forbidden topic in our Christian circles."

Mike was deeply attracted to another man at work, and they had fallen into sexual involvement. When an opportunity arose for him to take a different job in Oklahoma City, 150 miles away from where the Babbs lived in Wichita, Mike jumped at the chance. The family put their house up for sale. They planned for Beth and the kids to stay until it sold and then join Mike in Oklahoma.

Little did Beth imagine what lay ahead. The house never did sell. For the next eighteen months Beth and Mike saw one another only on weekends. In Oklahoma City, Mike found The First Stone, a Christian ministry dedicated to helping homosexuals find freedom. He attended its meetings regularly and began seeking God's healing.

Remarkable Growth

According to Beth, the changes over the next few months were remarkable. "Mike's growth was phenomenal. He had been depressed and hopeless, but became happy and full of hope. He regained a genuine desire to read his Bible and attend church, rather than simply going through the motions of being a Christian."

Meanwhile, Beth was also going through changes. After Mike left, she had to depend on God more than ever. Problems appeared around the house. First the washer broke, then the dryer, then the vacuum cleaner. A water hose burst and flooded the basement carpet and walls. Beth learned new meaning in the words "I can do everything through him who gives me strength" (Philippians 4:13). God became her "ever-present help in trouble" (Psalm 46:1), helping her figure out what to do in every crisis.

Beth and the children saw Mike on most weekends. Although she was praying for his restoration, she also felt a rising anger. "I tried to smile and encourage him, but inside I was seething. I couldn't wait for him to leave again. When he was gone, I didn't have to deal with him or the rejection I had felt when I learned he preferred a man to me."

When Mike eventually returned to Wichita, he went to see his pastor and told him the whole story. When others in the church found out, they were supportive and sympathetic. But Beth felt severely neglected. "It seemed that everyone took the attitude 'Poor Mike, look what he's been through.' I felt like a walking wound, but no one seemed to realize that I too had an injured heart."

Beth says the Lord was her only source of comfort. He began to teach her that his joy could be her strength (see Nehemiah 8:10). "God showed me that he would teach me how to be happy in spite of what was going on in my life. I began to keep my eyes, ears and heart open for every little thing that he wanted to bring to strengthen me." Some days she felt full of joy and hope. On others she would start to feel angry again.

One night the suppressed anger came rushing to the surface. Beth remembers the evening vividly: "Mike was out and did not return when he said that he would. I was reading a book, sitting on our bed. I looked at the clock and started to wonder whether he was off doing something 'strange and detestable.' I felt anger rising from the pit of my stomach, and I threw the book. Then I threw the pillows. It started to feel so good throwing things that I kept on doing it."

Lamps crashed to the floor, the ironing board flew across the room, laundry sailed everywhere. Beth flung flower arrangements, kitchen utensils, papers—everything she could get her hands on. Only exhaustion stopped her upheaval. Mike later came home with a reasonable explanation for his delay.

After that night, anger came pouring out of Beth at the slightest provocation. Anything could set her off—a disagreeable sales clerk, a rude driver, especially something Mike did. "I began having regular outbursts," she says. "Everyone who knew the 'sweet person' I had been was surprised. But no one was more surprised than me." Beth studied the Bible to see what God said about anger. "After reading every verse on anger I could find, I realized that if feeling angry was wrong, then God had a problem, because the Scriptures refer to his anger very often. I was relieved to know I was in good company!"

Beth realized, however, that sometimes her anger came out in destructive—and therefore sinful—ways. She began to pray for God's guidance in the right ways to release her emotions. She found help by writing about her feelings, admitting them in prayer and going for long walks. Gradually the anger subsided.

Today, almost ten years later, Beth's healing process continues. "God has brought me further than I ever believed possible," she says. "Respect for my husband has returned. God has also given me a willingness to help Mike in his ministry." Mike is director of Freedom at Last, a ministry of support to men and women leaving homosexuality.

Beth concludes, "God has given me the desire to see my life continually healed and changed. I know with complete confidence that my heavenly Father will finish the work that he has begun in me. I've seen him restore my husband and my marriage. There is nothing too hard for him."

A Friend in Need
Of course you don't have to be a parent or spouse to feel the effects of learning that someone you care about is gay. Close friends or relatives often have important questions and concerns. Perhaps you can relate to some of the issues that Sarah experienced in her friendship with Mary.

The two women met at a large denominational seminary where they were both part of the school's singles fellowship, a small group of about thirty men and women. Despite their age difference—Sarah was just out of college and Mary was in her early thirties—the two women hit it off almost immediately and cultivated their friendship by going on walks together.

During the year Sarah and Mary became good friends. Their long walks provided quality time together, and they enjoyed talking about almost every aspect of their lives, including their friendships with other students. Mary confessed that she had a crush on one of the "most eligible" bachelors in the student body. But as the months went by Mary spent an increasing amount of time discussing her friendship with another female student about ten years her senior.

"Their friendship had become very close," Sarah recalls. "To my mind, it seemed dependent. I was concerned—and somewhat confused—about the power that this relationship had over her life."

Rethinking Homosexuality

Then Mary took a basic counseling class which covered the issue of homosexuality. The female professor took the position that monogamous homosexual relationships were a valid alternative lifestyle for the practicing Christian. She encouraged her students to reexamine their beliefs on this issue.

Mary began doing a lot of reading about homosexuality from a variety of viewpoints. Was it acceptable theologically? Was it inborn? She had graduated from a conservative evangelical college prior to seminary. Now she was being challenged to rethink everything she believed about a subject that was causing conflicts in her own denomination.

"We spent a lot of time talking about homosexuality," says Sarah. "We discussed it from every angle, and even argued about the biblical texts." Mary wrote a paper that dealt with the various views on the subject and outlined principles of pastoral care for the person dealing with same-sex attractions.

Sarah began wondering if Mary's deep interest in the subject was more than academic. A short while later her suspicions were confirmed. Mary wrote a personal position statement on the issue, almost a history of her own sexual journey since adolescence. She talked about the significant relationships she'd had with various women throughout her life. One woman in particular, a family friend, had visited her family when Mary was a teenager. They would sleep in the same bed and cuddle, which Mary said was a powerful and positive experience for her.

Mary detailed strong connections she'd felt with other women. She had never consciously identified these strong bonds as sexual, but she could see a significant pattern of feeling love and deep affinity with other women. In the paper, she admitted she was probably a lesbian— or at least bisexual.

Mary showed Sarah this position paper. "I was somewhat shocked," Sarah remembers. "Although I'd seen it coming as a possibility, I kept hoping that Mary wasn't really lesbian. After all, she'd had a crush on this handsome single guy at school. And she'd recently gone out with another fellow, even becoming quite physically involved with him." Now Sarah wondered if Mary's current boyfriend had been one last attempt at heterosexuality.

"I was also scared," Sarah admitted, "knowing the kind of dependency she'd had with other women. Now I wondered if she felt that way toward me."

Outwardly, Sarah reacted with loving concern, telling Mary that she wasn't shocked, that she had seen this coming. She assured her that even though she disagreed with her stand on lesbianism, they would still remain friends.

Mary seemed relieved. She already knew Sarah's stand on the subject because they had spent so much time talking about it on a theoretical level. Suddenly Mary turned to Sarah and spoke softly. "Maybe you wonder if I feel this way about you."

Sarah could feel her pulse quicken. "Yes, it's crossed my mind."

"I could easily be attracted to you," Mary confessed. "But I'm not considering that an option because I know it's not your orientation. I know you're interested in Patrick."

Sarah admitted later that she found it "a little unnerving" to hear that Mary was attracted to her. At the same time, it was a relief to have these hidden questions out in the open where they could be honestly examined. And she was glad to sense an inner security about her own sexual identity, which was bolstered at the time by her serious dating relationship with Patrick, another seminary student.

Other Issues

In the following weeks Sarah had other issues to face. Mary asked her to tell no one about her confession, fearing that she might be kicked out of seminary. "I felt awkward about that," Sarah says, "and I was concerned that she would continue to hide it from her church. I also didn't want to see her go into a pastoral position without the church knowing. If it ever came out, it would probably split the church."

The two women spent a lot of time talking about these issues. Would it be ethical for Mary to have a lover and not tell the church she was pastoring? What if a lesbian accepted a pastoral position but was celibate? Sarah felt an increasing pressure from Mary to change her views on lesbianism. Finally, after both women realized that the other had carefully considered the issue from every angle, they agreed to respect the other's viewpoint without further arguments.

"I knew she had done a lot of reading," said Sarah, "and she had really wrestled with the Scriptures. I didn't agree with her, but I knew that she had carefully considered my views." Secretly, Sarah found herself still thinking, *Maybe if the right guy would just come along, it might sway her back.*

Then Mary was asked to leave her church for promoting a pro-gay position in her Sunday-school class for single adults. Within a short time, she was deeply involved at a pro-gay Metropolitan Community Church (MCC)—both in church activities and in a lesbian relationship with another female member. Eventually the women moved in together, partly in order to meet the requirements of living together for one year so that they could be "married" in an MCC ceremony.

During that year, Sarah and her fiancé, Patrick, made plans for their fall wedding. They wondered whether to invite Mary and her lover, worrying that the lesbian women might be openly affectionate and thus alienate the other wedding guests. After struggling with the options, they invited both women, who were discreet about their relationship during the whole event.

The following year Mary invited Sarah and Patrick to her gay wedding. Again, Sarah struggled to know the right response. Would her attendance be condoning immorality? Or would it simply imply that Mary was her friend who deserved support on a very important day in her life? Finally, after careful consideration, both Sarah and Patrick attended the MCC service.

Here's how Sarah explains that difficult decision: "From my perspective, this relationship seemed beneficial to Mary's life in many ways. It had been positive for her self-esteem and seemed to have many good dynamics, despite the fact that it was a lesbian relationship. Still, I did wonder whether or not it would last. And if it eventually did break up, I wanted to be there for Mary as a friend."

After Mary's wedding, she and her lover moved to another area of Minnesota, where Mary became a secretary at a small church that was open to gay members. Today, four years later, Sarah and Mary are still in contact, but only through occasional phone conversations.

"I don't regret my friendship with Mary at all," says Sarah. "Occasionally I find myself wondering, *What would so-and-so think if she knew that my best friend from seminary is now a practicing lesbian?* But most of the time I don't really think about it. Mary enriched my life in so many positive ways and certainly gave me a sensitivity to other Christians who are struggling with sexual identity issues."

The Challenge

These stories have raised many issues, some of them probably familiar to you. The following chapters will examine them in more detail so that you can get some insights into the perspective of your gay friend or relative and find specific ways to become a redemptive influence in his or her life.

2

The Grief Cycle: Surviving the Emotional Turmoil

*F*inding out about a gay child is agony," says Barbara Johnson. "It's almost like having a death in the family. But when someone dies you can bury that person and move on with your life. With homosexuality, the pain seems never-ending."

Barbara is speaking from firsthand experience. In 1968 her eighteen-year-old son joined the Marines and was killed in Vietnam. Exactly five years later, another son died in a head-on collision with a drunk driver. Barbara managed to move through these crises with her emotional health intact.

Then, on a hot June day in 1975, Barbara was on her way out the door when the phone rang. A friend of her twenty-year-old son Larry wanted to borrow a book, and Barbara went into his bedroom to find it.

Opening a desk drawer, she spotted the book and pulled it out. Hidden beneath was a stack of homosexual magazines. A wave of nausea swept over her. She managed to conclude the call, then hung up the phone in a daze of emotions.

She returned to Larry's room and fingered through the ads for gay films and other materials. Some of the literature was in envelopes, all addressed to her son at a post-office box in a nearby town. As the impact of the discovery hit her, Barbara was overwhelmed with a tidal wave of emotions.

"I threw myself down on the bed and a terrible roaring sob burst from me," she recalls in her autobiography, *Where Does a Mother Go to Resign?* "I was alone in the house, and for several terrifying minutes sobs from fear, shock and disbelief shook me. Flashing in my mind was this wonderful son who was so bubbly and happy—such a joy to have around. Thinking of him entwined with some other male brought heaves of heavy sobbing from deep wounds of agony."[1]

The Grief Cycle

Grief—often overwhelming and crippling—is the most common emotional reaction to the discovery of a loved one's homosexuality. This grief cycle has been described in many different ways. Figure 1 is one visual representation which many people have found helpful as they try to understand their reaction to this discovery.[2]

This "grief wheel" has four phases: shock, protest, disorganization, reorganization. Although some people move from one phase to the next in sequence, life is rarely that simple. It's not unusual to move back to a previous phase for a time. And it is extremely common to go through some phases more than once. For example, the initial discovery of a son's homosexual involvement may trigger a cycle of grief. Then his announcement that he has moved in with a male lover may cause another cycle. Years later, a diagnosis of AIDS could launch yet another.

As time passes, we move out of the cycle in one of two directions: deterioration or recovery.

Let's look at these phases of the grief cycle in more depth.

Loss: The "Trigger" to Grief

Grief is triggered when people experience a major loss in their life. It's

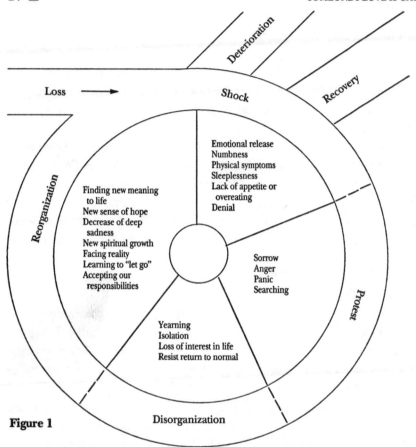

Figure 1

easy to understand this phenomenon when a dear friend or family member is diagnosed with a terminal illness or is accidentally killed. But why does learning of a loved one's homosexuality trigger such deep feelings? What exactly have you lost? You may be able to identify with a few of the following losses.

Loss of security. Even though your friend or relative has probably been aware of homosexual feelings for years, this is a new revelation to you. Suddenly you feel like you are talking to a stranger, as this unfamiliar aspect of their personality is revealed. The sense of betrayal can be devastating.

Perhaps you felt that yours was the "perfect" Christian marriage, or that your daughter was the epitome of mature godly womanhood. This was the son who never gave you a moment's trouble, or the one loyal friend who had been there for you when all others had failed. Now life has taken a strange turn in an unfamiliar direction, and you can feel extremely disoriented.

Loss of control. Suddenly life seems totally out of control. Your daughter has rejected Christianity, including the core moral values you have taught her since birth. Your husband has been unfaithful with another man; you feel disgusted and nauseated.

Events are pushing you in a direction you never thought you would be going. "If he was seeing another woman," one wife said, "I could fight it. But with this situation, I felt helpless—and totally lost."

Loss of future dreams. Before this discovery, the future may have seemed so bright and certain. Now you wonder what will happen to your family, your marriage, your children, your friends. Perhaps your son represented your one chance to experience the joy of being a grandmother. You always dreamed of your daughter's being the star of a huge "white gown" wedding in your family's church. You knew your husband would be a wonderful father, but now you can't believe he is leaving you. Your dreams have crashed on the hard rock of reality.

Loss of reputation. This can be a major issue, depending on your perceived "status" in the community or your local church. If you are a pastor, for example, you may feel insecure about your future employment opportunities. Or you are a parent and you thought you did a good job. What will people think of you now? And you feel so isolated. How can you tell anyone? They wouldn't understand!

Loss of relationship. Perhaps this is the core loss. The deeper the bond between you and this other person, the deeper your hurt on discovering their homosexuality. You know that the relationship has changed forever.

Whatever the exact losses you have experienced, the net result is the same: you are thrown into the initial stages of the grief cycle.

Initial Stage: Shock

For many people, the discovery of a loved one's homosexuality is the emotional equivalent of being hit over the head with a baseball bat.

Nothing was ever the same for me after Tony's confession. Much of my self-worth rested on the great job I had done in raising him single-handedly. Suddenly I was deeply ashamed of this son who had made me so proud the previous day. *What would people think of Tony if they knew?* I wondered. *And what would they think of me?* My son and I had been so close. *How could he do this to me?*

Many spouses react with similar deep emotions. One wife said she felt like a fragile heirloom vase which had been dropped. "I shattered into a million pieces inside."

You might experience several other symptoms of shock.

Emotional release. Right after the initial discovery might come a huge release of emotions. It's not unusual for a mother or wife to sob for hours, under a heaviness almost too painful to bear. Of course, the pain can be just as intense for men, whether or not they release it through tears. "On hearing the news," said one father, "I felt totally devastated and thorough-ly flattened. As I saw it, our nice, orderly family had been quietly going down the road of life, and suddenly we were hit by an express train!"[3]

Numbness. Some people react by going into a state of frozen emotions. They put one foot in front of the other, going through the motions like a zombie.

"My daughter was relieved by her confession of lesbianism," said one mother. "But I felt dead inside. My first thought was, *How can this happen in a Christian home? Doesn't God promise to protect our families from the really awful sins—like this one?*" Some mothers say this is their worst possible nightmare come true.

Numbness can function as God's shot of novocaine to help you bear up under the sudden knowledge of grievous sin in your loved one's life. This paralyzing dullness lessens the heavy load of a broken heart. Even-tually, as time passes, God will nudge you to begin facing the pain inside. Processing the hurt is the only way to release and resolve it.

Physical symptoms. All kinds of stress-related symptoms may appear: nausea, migraines, sleeplessness, lack of appetite and disinterest in mar-ital intimacy.

"When I found out, I was so nauseated that I threw up for three days," recalled one mother. "Every time I tried to be intimate with my husband, I couldn't stop thinking about what my son might be doing with his partner. The images in my mind were so awful that I couldn't function in my own marriage."

Often stress brings an inability to sleep, which can be detrimental to your health. Your days are filled with anxiety and nights bring complete exhaustion. If you sleep at all, you have disturbing dreams.

After tossing in bed for hours, Janice fell asleep, only to have dreams about wonderful times with her "pure" Christian daughter. They were laughing and sharing a loving intimate conversation—the way it used to be. Janice woke up with a smile on her face, which immediately was replaced by an inner stab of pain as she remembered that her precious daughter had left home to move in with a lesbian lover. Her dream seemed like a cruel joke God was playing on her; after repeated experiences like this, she began to fear going to sleep at all.

One mother has come to make the most of her sleepless nights. "Often I wake up in the middle of the night, unable to go back to sleep. But I have learned to use these times wisely. I try to anticipate them. I get to bed early when possible. I take naps when needed. I avoid disturbing movies or TV shows right before bedtime. I pray before I go to bed, that God will wake me when he wants me to spend some time with him in the night hours. I put my Bible, prayer list and journal by a comfortable chair, knowing that some of my best times with God have been in these wee hours of the morning."

The main thing to remember is that all these emotional and physical symptoms are typical for this type of stressful situation. You are *not* going crazy! These symptoms will diminish over time. You are normal, even healthy. It's much worse when all the emotions are "stuffed" inside, where they fester and remain unresolved.

Denial

Some family members, especially men, react by denying that any problem even exists. This can be caused by ignorance of homosexuality, or it can be a symptom of hoping for the best in a bad situation. When one wife confided to her husband about their son's homosexual activities, he retorted, "It's just a phase he's going through, honey. Don't worry so much. You always get so worked up about things!" With that pronouncement, he turned his attention back to the football game on television.

Denial is a form of instinctive protection, a way of coping with something too distressing to acknowledge. Sometimes it is a regular behavior pattern in a person's life.

Jenny called me because she found out that her husband was having some homosexual struggles. "I know he had a small problem in this area," she explained, "but that was long before we were married."

"What kind of problem did he have?" I asked.

"He was molested as a small boy, and that gave him thoughts of being with men. He also fooled around with some other boys in junior high. But that was many years ago."

When I asked how I could be of help, she replied, "He seems to be having some problems again. He's staying out all night, and he doesn't want sex with me. He's not even nice to me."

"Do you think he is having an affair?"

"Oh no," she said firmly. "I'm *sure* that's not the problem. But I think he is having problems with those thoughts again."

I could see that Jenny was trying to minimize her husband's problems. He was roaming the streets at night, and she had concluded that he was just *thinking* about having sex with other men. I suspected otherwise; later, my suspicions were confirmed. Jenny's husband began attending our ministry's weekly support group, and he admitted that he was involved in regular sexual activity with other men.

Without outside intervention, homosexuality or lesbianism is usually deep-rooted and persistent. Hoping that this issue will somehow resolve itself is unrealistic. Parents may think the problem is not really their child's but is due to companions who are exerting a bad influence. This is the reasoning that says, "He's not really gay; he caught it from his friends."

I fell into this deception when I found out about Tony and sent him to Oregon. I thought if I could just get my son away from his gay friends, everything would be fine. Several days later, my brother telephoned to announce that Tony had gone to church. I was overjoyed. God was answering my prayers—and so quickly!

Then my brother phoned again the next day. "Sorry, sis," he said in a flat voice. "You know that church Tony visited? Well, it's a gay church." My mind could not even process such a concept. A gay church? How could there be such a place? And how could Tony have found it so fast, and in such a small town?

Suddenly a new realization hit me full force: The problem wasn't Tony's friends. The problem wasn't Tony's location. The problem was Tony. I had spent all that money to get him far, far away—all for nothing!

Second Stage: Protest

In the second stage of the grief cycle, powerful emotions begin pouring forth. Although there may have been an emotional release when the discovery was first made, at this stage the intense emotional turmoil continues for weeks and months afterward. The pain is anguishing.

Sorrow. A tremendous outpouring of sorrow occurs, with tears that seem to last forever. "I'd sit at my desk at work, hoping no one would see the tears trickling down my face," recalls one mother. "I felt if I ever let go and really wept, I'd never be able to stop."

"It really hurt," admitted one father. "I wished I was dead. I wished my son was dead. And I wished that whoever got him into this in the first place was dead too."

Some people find themselves grieving at odd times, their emotions triggered by associations only they understand. A certain color of car, a particular city park or a specific restaurant may trigger important memories of the past, prompting a flood of tears.

"I remember sitting behind some young men in church who were about my son's age," recalled one mother. "They were laughing and joking with each other; they were so . . . normal. I began crying and ran out of church, sobbing my heart out."

Tears can bring healing and cleansing. Without a release, emotional pressure builds inside like a volcano getting ready to erupt. If you fear the tears pouring out at inappropriate times, find a safe place where you can give yourself permission to feel the pain, a private corner where you can express your fears. For some, this release can be shared with a close friend or counselor; others find themselves releasing sorrow in their times of private prayer.

Anger. It's normal to feel deep anger and even rage over this situation. How dare my son do this to me? How could my daughter throw away her Christian upbringing like this? Doesn't my husband care about how I feel? All my friend thinks about are her emotional needs—how selfish!

Carol saw this anger in her husband after they discovered their twenty-year-old son's homosexuality. Her husband would storm around the house yelling threats about what he would do to "the queer" who seduced their son into his first gay relationship. Carol felt she couldn't take it—first came her son's aberrant sexual behavior and now her husband's tirades. Finally she told him that *one* rebellious child in the family was enough, and he should act like an adult. Her rebuke quieted down her husband, but his anger did not go away.

Sometimes our anger is directed at God. We have had certain expectations of how our life would turn out, and homosexuality was certainly not in the script. We may have taught our child the Scriptures almost from birth. Doesn't God promise to protect the children of the godly? Or we have discovered that our husband has unresolved homosexual attractions dating back prior to marriage. Now we feel betrayed by God. We wonder, *If God knows everything, why did he let me marry this man?*

Panic. Some people are scared to death of others' reactions. Immediately they begin plotting how to keep this news a deep secret. They worry about the possible health consequences of immorality, especially the terrifying prospect of AIDS.

Suddenly homosexuality seems to be everywhere. The same day that Barbara Johnson found out about her son, her sister came to visit. When Barbara saw her purple luggage, she recalled a rumor that lavender is a favorite color among homosexuals. *Oh no, she's gay too!* she thought.

And the words *homosexuality . . . homosexuality . . . homosexuality* swirled in Barbara's head like a broken record.[4]

Searching. Many loved ones begin searching for a solution by contacting local pastors and Christian counseling centers. Parents can be very demanding because they are feeling out of control. They are desperate to save their child from harm. The quicker the solution, the better! Their focus becomes finding a solution to this overwhelming problem that has derailed their family life.

Sometimes parents are referred to an ex-gay ministry, and they call up to ask in desperation, "What can you send my son? He's not a Christian. Can you phone him and convince him to change?" They forget that the motivation to change must come from within—not as a persistent suggestion from well-meaning parents.

Unfortunately, many Christians have been deeply wounded by well-meaning counselors who give them bad advice—or no advice at all. Soon after I found out about my son's homosexual involvement, he ran away from home, and I decided to get counseling. I telephoned the large church my brother attended and decided to warn them ahead of time why I was coming.

"My son is a homo . . . my son is a homo . . ." I choked on the word, and the receptionist kept asking me to speak up. Finally I got the truth out, and she didn't seem shocked at all—much to my relief. *At least now they'll know why I'm coming,* I thought, *and they will have the best person available to help me.*

When my brother and I walked into this church's counseling department, I feared that everyone would point at us or whisper behind our backs. The lady behind the counter handed me a pink card to fill out. It asked the reason for my visit, but neither my brother nor I knew how to spell the word *homosexual.*

When a nice young man came out to get us, he looked busy. As we sat down in his office, he glanced down at the card. A flash of panic crossed his face. I realized he had no idea why we had come. The rest of our session is a blur. I know he wanted to say the right things, but he was obviously far out of his comfort zone. He fumbled through his

Bible and read us some verses condemning homosexuality. Not exactly what a desperate mother and her brother needed at the moment!

I remember asking him what I should do about my sixteen-year-old son who had run away from home. He advised me to leave him alone and let the Lord deal with him. After a brief prayer we left. My mind was still full of unanswered questions. I could almost see our counselor breathing a huge sigh of relief as we made our exit.

Stage Three: Disorganization

The third stage of the grief process may take weeks or even months. The immediate shock is gone, and the emotional outbursts have eased off. Now it's almost as if our whole emotional being goes into hibernation and we are on "hold," fixated on this one issue. The inner pain seems never-ending and too deep for words.

Externally, things may fall apart. *Why does it matter if my house is a wreck?* a mother will wonder. *My son is gay!* Often the normal activities of life which previously brought such joy seem totally irrelevant, even frivolous. Nothing is important anymore.

Yearning. We experience a deep emotional longing for "the way things used to be." In reality, our family relationships may not have been good, but they *seemed* good at the time—or at least better than now. I can remember thinking, *If only we had not moved to the town where that counselor came into Tony's life* . . . But later I was able to see the truth: that counselor did not turn my son into a homosexual. Tony had problems in his life long before that day. This realization enabled me to take my sorrow to God and let him heal it. Gradually I began to look forward again, rather than spending all my time longing for the "good old days." Facing the truth about the past gave me the courage to move on.

Isolation. Knowing of our loved one's homosexuality can put us into an extremely awkward situation. "How is your son doing these days?" is such a natural question. But what should we say? That he's "fine"? That he's "busy with his new career"? Some parents conclude that the awkward questions are avoided most easily by staying away from the people—such as friends at church—who have a tendency to ask them.

One father said, "I went into my 'cave,' the garage where I do my woodwork. I avoided everyone. I stopped going to the men's group at church because I was so ashamed."

"It seemed like no one could possibly know how I felt," recalled one mother. "So I withdrew totally, and spent all day in front of the television. I threw gigantic pity parties which lasted for days. Unfortunately, no one came but me!"[5]

"I didn't talk about this with anyone—except my wife—for a long time," said one father. "I was extremely disappointed. But I stuffed down my feelings. Every time I thought about it, I wondered what we could have done differently—and what we could do now. It really helped when my wife and I became part of a group of parents dealing with the same thing."

The situation becomes even more tense when the person struggling with homosexuality swears others to secrecy. The issues of isolation and disclosure are so important that we will examine them in more depth in chapter four.

Loss of interest in life. It's common to lose interest in the other events of daily life upon finding out about someone's homosexuality.

"I obsessed on that one issue," said Jane, whose boyfriend told her about his struggles after she pressed him for a deeper commitment in their dating relationship. "I couldn't think about anything else when I thought of John."

As we focus on this one issue, we may stop doing other things that could actually help us move through the pain. Our obsession with our loved one cuts us off from other meaningful relationships. People are depending on us, particularly if we are married with a family, but we become incapable of meeting their needs. So others become a sacrifice on the altar of our wayward child.

Resist returning to normal. In this phase of grief, we may resist resuming normal activities. How can we move on with life? Should we accept the fact that things will never be quite the same again? Does that mean we are giving up hope? "How can God expect me to go on," one mother asked, "just living as though nothing had happened? How can I return to normal? Nothing will ever be normal again!"

If we get stuck in this stage of pain and immobility, we become like the demanding child who holds his breath, trying to force his parents to yield to his demands. Our attitude says, "God, I want you to fix this problem—right now! And I'm not going to budge until you do." God is vitally concerned about your loved one's struggles—and your own pain as a result—but experience has taught all of us working in this field of ministry that circumstances rarely change as fast as we'd like. God does not "fix" this problem according to our timetable.

A child's decision to seek help rarely comes quickly. Long-term change comes as the result of a deep commitment, which takes time to develop. And the primary motivation must come from that person—not from a loved one. Most ex-gay ministries will refuse to contact your loved one directly, especially if he or she is not interested in help. Over the years, we have found that such an approach is virtually useless, and occasionally brings us an angry threat of a lawsuit for invasion of privacy.

Stage Four: Reorganization

Eventually, like a deep wound that heals, our feelings of being emotionally "raw" begin to disappear. Like a bear coming out of hibernation, we feel alive again in ways that have been absent for months. The scattered pieces of our life begin to fall into place again. We have passed into the phase that we call "reorganization." What are some characteristics of this stage?

Decrease of deep sadness. One day we wake up and recognize that the internal weight of grief has decreased. Perhaps we will realize one afternoon that it has been several hours since we have thought about our loved one's situation.

"I can remember having several hours, then several days, go by without this huge wave of sorrow sweeping over my life," one mother recalled. "Soon my joy began to return. I was so excited. The air seemed fresher, the sunshine brighter, and I even recaptured my sense of humor. I felt alive again!"

Finding hope again. Another sign of healing is the presence of hope.

We no longer dread the future; we sense that good things can still be ahead. When we are weak and afraid, we can be honest with God. He says in 2 Corinthians 12:9 that his power shows up best in weak people. That is wonderful to know! Another verse that encourages me is Psalm 31:24: "Be strong and take heart, all you who hope in the LORD." This passage reminds me that my hope is not dependent on the shifting circumstances around me but on something unchangeable: the character of God and his love for me. I can draw inner peace and strength from remembering this truth.

New spiritual growth. As we move through our grief, we have an opportunity to stretch our spiritual muscles. They may be flabby, but we can exercise our faith daily. We can choose to walk one day at a time, not looking ahead into the future. This is what Jesus meant when he said, "Do not worry about tomorrow, for tomorrow will worry about itself. Each day has enough trouble of its own" (Matthew 6:34). We do not have the grace to bear the burdens of tomorrow; the load we are carrying today is all we can handle right now.

As we emerge from grief, we may be surprised with a sense of new inner strength. Just as a tree endures through a hard and bitter winter season, then emerges with new vigor and growth, this situation gives us the opportunity to grow emotionally and spiritually.

We have had to trust God in a whole new way because we have come face-to-face with a problem that we cannot fix ourselves. Since finding out about my son, I have turned to God in deep sorrow, great fear and intense frustration. Often he gives me *just* the comfort and direction that I have needed for the situation. Then I can trust him even more the next time a problem arises.

One morning I was praying about a situation that filled me with grief. Then, in reading my Bible, I came across John 16:33, where Jesus is speaking to his disciples. He tells them, "I have told you these things, so that in me you may have peace. In this world you will have trouble. But take heart! I have overcome the world." These words encouraged me. Troubles will come, Jesus said, but he can give us peace in the midst of trying circumstances. When we learn how to put that principle into practice, we grow spiritually as a result.

Facing reality. We acknowledge that things will never be quite the same again. Life has changed forever. We will never view our loved one with the same eyes of innocence again. Although this fact is painful, we must accept it and grapple with its implications.

As we gain a new spiritual awareness, we are able to face the future as it really is. Our loved one may not come "back into the fold," at least as soon as we'd like. But we can go on with our life, even while knowing that our loved one is making wrong choices. Usually by this time, we have tried everything humanly possible to get them straightened out! We are left with no other choice but to release our circumstances to God. Eventually we can use what God has shown us to reach out to others who are hurting. We begin to find some good in a bad situation (see 2 Corinthians 1:3-4).

Learning to let go. In this phase we begin to release our past hopes, knowing that many of them will never come true. While our particular issue is homosexuality, this principle covers a wide range of situations.

Most parents face deep disappointment of some kind in one or more of their children's lives. Their pain is similar to what we have felt; our hurt is not unique. As parents, we still have hope for the future and we long to see our children succeed in life. But we cannot control their destiny; they alone are responsible for their future choices. We can be an influence for good, but not a police officer who forces them to obey our wishes.

When Tony reached the age of eighteen, I had to face the fact that he didn't need me in the same way he had previously. That's a turning point faced by every parent. During his teens, he had begun leaving his Christian faith and embracing a wild lifestyle—a common situation in many families. His claiming a homosexual identity was an excruciating situation for me, but many parents have faced a crisis of similar devastation.

Wives must face this reality too. The fact that your husband has committed adultery with another man is crushing. But it is not too different from what other wives—maybe some in your own church—have gone through with errant husbands who have fallen into heterosexual adultery.

Accepting our responsibilities. Moving through grief includes accepting responsibility for our past mistakes and seeking wisdom for doing the right thing now. Dealing with guilt—whether real or imagined—is such a huge issue that we will discuss it in detail in the next chapter.

"One day I had a big revelation," one wife admitted. "I realized that all our family problems were *not* caused by my husband's sexual struggles." This wife realized that she had been "mothering" her husband—a common pattern. "I was upset that we were having difficulties in our sexual relationship. Then another wife counseled me, 'If you treat him like a bad little boy during the day, he will find it difficult to act like a man when he comes to bed with you.' That really hit me between the eyes."

Other family members—including ourselves—may be contributing to problems in the home. Are we responding to this crisis in appropriate ways? For example, the fact that my daughter is pursuing lesbianism doesn't give me the license to gain fifty pounds or blow the family budget with wild shopping sprees. By honestly facing our own problem areas, we are better able to work through this situation successfully.

Moving Beyond Grief

Sometimes we move through certain stages of grief more than once. New circumstances will trigger that old feeling of being overwhelmed by sorrow. This is normal, and most of us go through this process more than once. As our lives proceed, however, the waves of grief will diminish. We will not be knocked so far down, and the recovery time will be shorter.

That's what usually happens. Some people, however, get trapped in an endless cycle of grief; as time goes on, they sense that things are actually getting worse. The person who cannot surrender this situation to God may sink slowly into bitterness. It's easy for this to occur. There is a narrow line between believing in faith that God will change someone, and trying to manipulate that person to change. If we become too disillusioned, we may abandon Christianity altogether.

I have been involved in numerous parents' groups over the past fifteen years. Sharon came to one of my groups soon after finding out about her son. She was an emotional wreck and grabbed on to our support like a drowning woman clutching a life preserver.

Sharon listened eagerly to my teachings each week and soon was entering into the discussion. She devoured every piece of literature, especially the testimonies of men and women who had been set free. Soon she was so cheerful at meetings that she became a special encouragement to all the other parents.

Then, after several months had passed, Sharon hit a crisis point. Her son wasn't enthusiastic about the literature she passed on to him. Her long hours of prayer appeared to have no effect on his behavior. Slowly I noticed that Sharon was withdrawing; she was less cheerful and had less to contribute. Soon she had dropped out of the meetings altogether.

A few months later I was visiting her neighborhood and decided to stop by for a quick visit. When she answered the door, I was stunned. Her brown eyes were dull, almost glazed. Deep wrinkles lined her face. Her clothes were disheveled. She looked ten years older than when I had last seen her.

Sharon told me that she didn't care anymore what her son did. When I tried to comfort her, she was unresponsive. When I mentioned the Lord, she seemed indifferent. She mouthed the "correct" responses to my spiritual questions, but I could tell that she was only going through the motions. I felt like I was talking to a stone wall; after a few minutes of conversation, I left.

I was so uncomfortable being around Sharon that I never went back. I was shocked at the total deterioration in her appearance. I was secretly relieved to get away. Now, many years later, I am still haunted by the empty look in her eyes. Sharon had given up hope—both in her son *and* in God. Her plans, especially her timetable of expectations, had been different from God's, and she had grown weary in waiting.

I have faced similar situations since that day, and I have not been quite as surprised when they occurred. I have learned to allow these mothers to vent their feelings without receiving quick advice from me. I try to see behind their words and respond to the pain: "I can really understand how hurt and disappointed you are right now." Such a sympathetic response can prompt a flood of tears, and I respond by holding the person in my arms. Ideally we can also pray together, which offers a chance for the mother to pour out her pain to the only One who can heal the deep hurt that she carries inside.

Getting "Unstuck"

Sharon's situation is not unique. For others it has been a long time since they found out about this situation in their family. Yet they are still deep in an endless pit of despair. What are some long-term symptoms they may be experiencing?

☐ Decreased energy. No matter how much they rest, they are always devoid of energy.

☐ Sleep disturbance. Some sleep all the time, while others can't get any sleep. Or, after sleeping a few hours, they are wide awake and can't get back to sleep. Both patterns lead to feeling "always tired."

☐ Change in appetite. Some will look to food as a source of comfort; others will lose their appetite completely.

☐ Sense of worthlessness. They feel that nothing will ever change. They have somehow failed. Life is hopeless.

☐ Thoughts of suicide. They begin to imagine that ending their life would be easier than continuing to feel the despair of their present circumstances.

For these people, prolonged despair has led to the symptoms of a clinical depression. These feelings are normal if they last several months. If they persist, however, they may need specialized help. Here are three practical suggestions that have helped others get beyond depression:

Get a thorough physical exam. Prolonged stress can cause alterations in your body chemistry. Get a complete physical examination from your physician. Let him or her know that you are particularly concerned about any underlying physical problems that may be prolonging your period of despair.

Find several people to give you regular emotional support. One common reason a person gets stuck in grief is that he or she has been bearing burdens alone. Perhaps you have told a few others but they have not understood or been deeply empathic. Maybe your husband knows but is not dealing with this situation in the same way. Whatever the reasons, you are not getting the emotional support that is vitally important to recovery. If this is true for you, it's time to find additional help. Consider a pastor, trained therapist or specialized ex-gay ministry with expertise in addressing the needs of parents. You need an outlet for your emotions, and this can come through talking about your situation with someone else on a regular basis. I have a wooden plaque hanging in my bathroom which says, "Friendship doubles our joy and divides our grief." I have found my close friends to be the greatest gift during the hard times.

Consider taking antidepressants. In the past there has been great shame attached to taking medication for depression. In his book *Why Do Christians Shoot Their Wounded?* psychiatrist Dwight Carlson says, "In my experience Christians are intolerant, if not prejudiced, against individuals with emotional difficulties. Most view all such problems as due to personal sin."[6]

Fortunately this stigma is passing, Carlson says, and increasing numbers of dedicated Christians are finding help with emotional difficulties through antidepressants. Medication, of course, will not solve the underlying reasons for your depression, but it will enable you to begin experiencing more normal emotions while you seek counseling to resolve the deeper issues.

Stand Against Condemnation

In the Christian world, depression is sometimes seen as a sign of failure resulting from an inability to trust God. But the Bible shows that some of the most celebrated biblical figures suffered from times of great discouragement.

After defeating the prophets of Baal and being threatened by Queen Jezebel, Elijah ran for his life by escaping into the desert. He was so discouraged that he prayed to die. "I have had enough, LORD," he said. "Take my life" (1 Kings 19:4). Men and women greatly used by God were not immune to times of great despair. Other Bible passages are also an excellent resource in dealing with depression. In particular, the psalms have been a comfort to depressed people in every age.

It's often difficult for us to admit that we need help. I remember going in to see my doctor for a physical a few years ago when I was caring for Rick, my son's partner of ten years who was terminally ill with AIDS. I really needed some help. I couldn't sleep. After the exam I was talking to the doctor in her office and casually asked her for some medication to help me sleep. I didn't let the doctor know anything about my life or why I was having problems with insomnia. Probably I feared looking weak or losing control of my emotions in her office. I didn't get the needed help, because she couldn't see past my pasted-on smile.

So I encourage you to *be real*. Let someone know you need help! Whether it's help with sleeping or finding emotional support, don't be self-sufficient like me in the doctor's office. I've had to learn that being weak is not a negative thing. Remember, God says that only through our weakness will we know his strength.

That's a truth that Barbara Johnson has learned. After finding the gay magazines in her son's room, she confronted him—and twenty-year-old Larry disowned his family and disappeared into a homosexual lifestyle. After almost a year of deep depression, Barbara had a breakthrough. "Whether Larry kills himself," she told God, "or if I never see him again—whatever, Lord—he is yours." She had said it many times before, but this time she felt relief from the crushing grief. "My teeth stopped itching and the elephant got off my chest for the first time in almost a year."

After another decade of silence punctuated by periodic contact, Barbara's son visited her in May 1986. "I want you to forgive me for the eleven years of pain I've caused you," he said with tears in his eyes. "I've rededicated my life to the Lord. I'm released from that bondage I was in, and God has really cleansed me. Now I can stand clean before the Lord."[7] Today his mother travels widely, encouraging other parents through her speaking engagements and bestselling books.

Barbara says that because of Christ's death for us all, there is always hope—no matter what our life's circumstances. "God is offering Himself to you daily, and the rate of exchange is fixed. It is your sins for His forgiveness, your tragedy and hurt for His balm of healing, and your sorrow for His joy."[8]

3
Guilt:
The Continual
Crushing Weight

*G*uilt *is epidemic in our culture, the driving force in many people's lives.*
Some families run on guilt. It can be used as a great motivator. Parents
use guilt on their children to manipulate behavior, and children use it
on their parents for the same reason.

But the main focus of this chapter is not the guilt that others heap on
us, nor the guilt that we might project toward others. It's the guilt that
threatens to overcome us in waves when we find out that our loved one
is gay. This is especially true for parents and spouses, but it can also be
a big factor in close friendships, especially those that have spanned
many years.

Parents: Prime Candidates
Parents are the prime candidates for guilt. To their anguish, a child has
gone astray. Soon they are stuck in the "if only" syndrome: If only they
had been a better parent . . . if only they had become a Christian earlier

in life . . . if only they had lived their faith more consistently . . . The list is endless. Thousands of condemning thoughts plague our minds when things derail. Suddenly we are filled with insights on how we could have (perhaps) prevented this latest tragedy.

There are specific issues around which parents feel guilt. Let's look at the most common.

"I was an imperfect parent." This is true. But *all* parents make mistakes. So welcome to the human race! You are no different from any other parent. And let's face the facts here: some kids from the worst homes come out smelling like a rose.

All of us have read stories of abused or underprivileged children who have grown up to become famous surgeons, lawyers or pastors. Against all odds, these kids have survived and gone on to make a huge success of their lives. Obviously their fathers are not sitting at home, feeling guilty about their poor upbringing. These dads are probably boasting to everyone who will listen about their famous children and their latest list of accomplishments. No room for guilt here.

We also hear about the child from the "perfect" home who has dropped out of high school and now has been arrested for using illegal drugs. How is that person's mother coping? Probably she is wrestling with guilt over all her "mistakes" that resulted in her child's problematic behavior. She may also be angry, muttering statements that end with the phrase "after all I did for you."

Parents of homosexual children carry a lot of shame. Despite the huge gains that have been made in terms of pro-gay activism, the majority of people in our society still disapprove of homosexuality. And parents share the stigma of their child's sexual behavior. This is especially true for parents who are members of a conservative Christian church. In many churches homosexuality is right up there with the biggest sins imaginable—or so it feels to parents who have just discovered this situation within their family. Of course, contrary to our cultural norms, the Bible does not "grade" sins on a scale of bad to worse. All sin separates us from God (Romans 3:23), and Jesus died for them all.

"I caused my child's homosexuality." This statement is totally false and is

probably the biggest lie you will have to stand against. *No one person has the power to cause another's homosexuality.* At worst, a parent-child relationship may be *one factor* in a whole complex group of influences.

So it's not fair to blame parents as *the* cause for their child's homosexuality. At the same time, some parents go to the other extreme and insist that family factors have absolutely nothing to do with their child's struggles. Actually the truth lies somewhere in between, and the situation is different for every family.

We cannot avoid the important question, What causes homosexuality? There is a great deal of focus these days on studies which point toward a genetic cause. But homosexuality cannot possibly be solely genetic in its origins. The idea is easily disproved by looking at studies involving identical twins. If homosexuality is purely genetic, identical twins would always share the same sexual orientation, whether heterosexual or homosexual. But this is not what occurs. In one widely publicized study, when one identical twin was homosexual, the other was also gay only about half the time.[1] So other factors must be at work here.

Many researchers have concluded that environmental factors contribute to homosexuality, even if some kind of inborn factors also exist.[2] At this point in the discussion, most parents begin to cringe. If homosexuality can be caused—even partially—by environmental factors, parents know they have been an important part of their child's environment.

But here we must make another important distinction. As Christians, we know that children are subject to all kinds of temptations toward sinful thoughts and activities. If certain environmental factors make some children vulnerable to homosexual feelings, that child still chooses whether or not to act on those impulses.

Further, a child can become vulnerable to homosexual feelings due to factors over which a parent has little or no control. Many gay men report feeling "different" from earliest childhood. Sometimes these feelings originate from a physical factor (e.g., being shorter than average height). Sometimes the child's personality, lack of coordination or other circumstances can cause feelings of loneliness.

These factors can lead, in turn, to peer rejection. The child who is picked on by peers can suffer deep wounds. Name-calling may soon follow, with hurtful labels like "sissy" and "fag" for the boys, "lesbo" and "dyke" for the girls. These labels can take root in the hearts of children who are already feeling insecure.

An overwhelming majority of lesbians—and a significant number of gay men—have been victims of sexual abuse. In women, this can lead to a deep-seated fear and/or hatred of men; in men, it can lead to a profound confusion about their masculinity. Parents may have no knowledge of this devastation that is occurring in their child's life. In many cases, abused children hide their feelings for fear of rejection by even the most loving parent.

Sometimes a parent is absent from the family because of unfortunate circumstances, such as death or divorce. Other times, the parent is present but the child perceives a rejection or lack of love which in fact does not exist. These are just a few examples of environmental and relational factors which can push someone toward a homosexual identity and which have little—if anything—to do with a parent's actions.

Spouses and Less-Than-Ideal Marriages

Just as there are no perfect parents, there are no perfect marriages. If a marriage goes sour and a husband or wife becomes involved in adultery, both spouses feel guilty—whether their mistakes are real or imagined.

Even the best of homes often does not compare well with the spiritual ideal presented in some churches. We hear about the model of a loving father who cherishes his wife as his own flesh. Mom joyfully submits to Dad's leadership, and both delight in raising their family. Their young cherubs sit in silent rapture as Dad reads from the Bible each night in front of the crackling fireplace . . . No, each of us can find lots of room for guilt in comparing our marriages with this idealized fantasy.

Husbands and wives facing homosexuality within their marriage hear all kinds of guilt messages inside their mind.

"I was a poor wife (husband)." One husband felt this crisis must be all his fault. His wife had special needs which he was unaware of, he rea-

soned. But husbands and wives facing this situation are usually no better or worse than thousands of other married men and women whose marriages are holding together.

Usually a wife begins to feel uneasy even before she knows the exact nature of her husband's struggles. She senses something wrong but does not know what. She wonders if she is really meeting her husband's needs. *If I were a better wife, he would stay home more,* she thinks, feeling guilty for not keeping a cleaner home, staying slimmer or being more available sexually. Meanwhile, her husband may be looking for any excuse he can to be away from the house to pursue casual sex with other gay men. In extreme cases, a husband might even pick fights with his wife in order to have an excuse to slam out of the house in a fit of rage— and head for the nearest gay bar.

"I caused my husband's (wife's) homosexuality." This accusation is totally far-fetched. Although a wife may feel responsible, she did not create the problems brought into the marriage by her husband. Similarly, a husband must realize that he is not responsible for his wife's childhood hurts.

Sometimes a spouse will acknowledge that he or she did not cause the homosexual inclinations, but will feel guilty over actions that may have pushed the spouse toward acting them out.

Bill was a young pastor who became so preoccupied with his new church that his home life began to suffer. His wife, Beth, felt isolated in the new community, with no time to make new friends because her three preschool children were at home all day. Then a young woman came into the church who needed counseling and emotional support. She had just come through a divorce and was depressed. Bill was delighted when his wife began spending time with her, even when their relationship began taking his wife away from home in the evenings. But when the house began to look unkept and the dirty laundry piled high, Bill began feeling uneasy.

One evening, when Beth headed out for the third night in a row to spend "just a few hours" with her new friend, Bill confronted her. Although at first she would not admit it, eventually Beth confessed that their relationship had turned into an emotional dependency, then the two women had become sexually involved with each other. Bill's church ministry was beginning to soar, but his marriage was crashing down around him.

Friends and Guilt

Friends can also struggle with guilt, although usually not to the same extent as parents or spouses. They wonder if their actions somehow pushed their friend into this new sphere of immorality. A friend may wonder, *If only I had acted differently, maybe I could have prevented this tragedy.*

Janice had strong romantic feelings for a young man who was a family friend. Their parents often spent time together, so Janice and Don saw each other at family functions.

Don had seemed to ignore her for a long time, but then he began showing her more and more attention. Before long, they were spending a lot of time alone together, and when Don asked Janice to marry him, she accepted.

But Janice began picking up little clues that something was wrong. Don seemed somehow distant, even when they were alone. Janice noticed that he was far more interested in hanging around his male friends than being with her. She confronted him with these things.

Don was adamant that he should be able to spend as much time with his friends as he wanted. He denied that anything was wrong. Janice continued to feel uneasy and finally broke off the engagement.

Don's parents were very upset with her, and she felt guilty—but also relieved. Several days later, one of her cousins told her a secret among some of the family: Don was a practicing homosexual, and certain family members had hoped that his romance with Janice would be the answer to his problems.

In the months that followed, Janice heard that Don had plunged even deeper into immorality with other men after their breakup. She struggled with guilt. Was it her fault that Don had become even more involved with men? Had she destroyed his only chance for a normal married life?

Finding True Resolution

Guilt can be a huge issue to deal with, especially for those who are closest to the homosexual loved one. Some people resolve their sense of guilt by revising their beliefs about homosexuality. Parents—even Christians—begin to reject the biblical position that homosexual behavior is sin (see Leviticus 18:22; Romans 1:24-27; 1 Corinthians 6:9-11). Now they believe that God created homosexual men and women, and therefore same-sex relationships are normal. Soon these parents are marching with their children in gay-rights parades.

One mother, a lifelong churchgoer, learned about her son's homosexuality. After searching the Scriptures and doing much reading, she revised her long-held views on this subject. Within months she was attending a local pro-gay church and affirming same-sex marriages. Any guilt she had felt over her son's situation was gone. But did she resolve her guilt—or only hide it behind false rationalizations?

The Bible consistently forbids sexual activity outside of a lifelong heterosexual commitment. So we must reject the pro-gay reinterpretations of Scripture. It's beyond the scope of this book to delve further into this issue, but excellent resources can provide further study in this area.[3]

Avoiding the truth does not resolve guilt. So what is the solution? Boldly facing the truth, then walking through the guilt to repentance and forgiveness. This of course can be a deeply painful process. It can be very hurtful, for example, to hear your gay loved one's true feelings about his or her upbringing. That person walks away feeling great for having "vented," and you are left looking for a safe place to fall apart. The Scriptures say that "the truth will set you free" (John 8:32). That's true, but there can be a lot of turmoil to endure first.

Dealing with the truth of my son's reasons for getting involved in homosexuality has been a great challenge for me. It has become a lot easier since I established a safe place to vent my own feelings. In my private times with God, I can release the hurt, guilt and sorrow to him. Then I experience his comfort and forgiveness.

As mentioned earlier, no explanation fits every family. The truth is different for each situation. So how can we discover the truth for our family? A few specific steps may help.

Seek insights on the past. In attempting to uncover the truth, be open to hear how your past actions have affected your loved one who has turned to homosexuality. Discussing the whole situation with other family members or a Christian counselor can bring additional insights. Ask the Lord to give you understanding through his Word and during your times of prayer concerning this family member or friend. A simple yet wonderful prayer is "Lord, speak to me." When our hearts are open, the Word of God may convict us, but it also comes alive with comfort and hope.

Pray for the right timing and situation to ask your gay loved one directly. Find a time to talk privately. Here is a possible opening statement: "Because of my love for you, I've been trying to educate myself on the subject of homosexuality. Many researchers believe that family dynamics can contribute to this situation. If this is true for our family, I'd like to hear your insights." Close the conversation by leaving the door open for future discussion: "I want you to know that you can talk to me more about this subject anytime."

Sometimes individuals dealing with homosexuality have a clear idea of the family factors that caused deep emotional wounds. Many gay men, for example, confess that they never felt an emotional identification with their fathers. "Dad did his best," they say, "but he was always so involved with his job that I felt like he was not interested in me at all." Or a lesbian woman will confess to being forced by a male relative into incest, which led her to avoid all intimacy with men. Pray that God will provide opportunities for you and your loved one to discuss these issues in an open and loving way.

Seek insights on homosexuality. Learn the basics about homosexuality. Many excellent Christian books can help you learn more about this issue (see appendix A). Although many of them are directed at the person overcoming homosexuality, they will help you understand the problems your loved one must face in order to find genuine freedom. Understanding the "root" emotional issues underlying the homosexual drive will give you deep insights into your loved one's life and help you pray in more specific ways for the whole situation.

Seek a new start for the future. You cannot change the past—but you can change the impact of the past. It's never too late to begin laying a new foundation for your future relationship with your loved one.

No matter what your relationship—or lack of one—has been like in the past with this person, begin praying that God will open up a new chapter in your relationship. Old patterns are difficult to overcome, but God is the God of the impossible. "I am the LORD, the God of all mankind. Is anything too hard for me?" (Jeremiah 32:27).

Who Is Responsible?

One important principle has freed many family members from a sense of false guilt: Remember who is responsible for your loved one's life. *You cannot control your loved one's choices—only your reaction to their choices.* You cannot be guilty for things over which you have no control. And you have no control over the moral choices of your adult children. Whatever factors may or may not have contributed to their present circumstances, God will hold them responsible for the decisions they make as adults. "The soul who sins is the one who will die. The son will not share the guilt of the father, nor will the father share the guilt of the son" (Ezekiel 18:20). All of us have unresolved issues from our past; all of us are morally responsible for how we seek to resolve those issues.

Remember Bill, the pastor whose wife left him for another woman because she was so emotionally needy? This situation is more common than some realize. Often a wife with lesbian tendencies has never been involved in a sexual relationship with another woman before her wedding day. But she comes into her marriage with many emotional needs that her husband can't meet or understand. Her neediness may actually drive her husband away, prompting her to fulfill her emotional needs in sinful ways.

Bill realized that he had let his wife down. He hadn't known how to help her, and he had tried to separate himself from her demands. He needed to confess this and ask her forgiveness. At the same time, he could not take responsibility for the problems she had brought into the marriage or for her choice to pursue a lesbian relationship.

Bill was able to sort out what he was responsible for—and what he was not. As Bill took responsibility for his failures, he was able to see clearly what course of action to pursue. He could also start dealing with the anger he felt toward his wife's adultery, and eventually extend a hand of forgiveness and reconciliation.

What about Janice, the young woman who broke off with her homosexual fiancé? Her romance with Don would have led to a problem-filled marriage. Because he had not resolved the root issues behind his behavior, he would certainly have continued his same-sex immorality after marriage. His choices were destroying his life. And they would have destroyed Janice's happiness too. Eventually she resolved her feelings of guilt, confident that Don's moral choices were not her responsibility.

Sadness, Not Guilt

A second principle helps many people deal with guilt: Remember that guilt is different from sadness. We can claim freedom from the guilt of our past actions, but we can still be sad for the ongoing consequences of those actions.

Ironically, as I have accepted the sorrow over my past, I've found peace. Beneath the pain, there is a foundation of joy. I still experience deep sadness over my son's situation, but my joy and peace run even deeper. I love 2 Corinthians 6:10 in the Living Bible paraphrase, which says, "Our hearts ache, but at the same time we have the joy of the Lord." God's peace can comfort us at a deeper level than the emotional turmoil.

Because of painful experiences in my own life, I have been able to reach out with empathy to other people in deep pain. Does that make my pain worth it? No. But it has made my pain *worthwhile*. There's a big difference.

Dealing with Guilt Relapse

It's one thing to know that forgiveness is available; it's another matter altogether learning how to experience that forgiveness. We can know the truth in our mind, but our heart is still breaking. How can we deal with the pain when overwhelming guilt crushes us again and again?

I have struggled with this cycle, not just when I found out initially that Tony was gay, but periodically since then. I will be free of guilt for a while, only to have it hit all over again with renewed force. I have accepted God's forgiveness for things I did wrong, but years later found myself still feeling guilty.

Even though I conceived my son out of wedlock, I loved him before his birth and couldn't give him up. I knew that he deserved a good home; I was only nineteen but determined to be the perfect mother. Tony was a beautiful baby, the joy of my life. As the months passed, I was so proud to be the mother of this bright little toddler.

Then reality set in. I had to stay home and be a mom while my friends went out and partied. My life was filled with maternal responsibilities, while others could be spontaneous and carefree. Being a mother didn't seem fun after all, and I began to resent my situation. It didn't help that I was stuck in a tiny one-room apartment.

I tried keeping up with my friends, but that didn't work. They could stay out all night; I had to be home or pay the baby sitter. They could drink and sleep it off the next morning while I had to get up and go to a boring job.

I became a Christian when Tony was five, but a lot of bad influences had already taken root in his little mind. Although things improved after that, we still had many difficulties to work through as Tony got older and I had no husband to support me in raising him.

Then came the awful discovery that Tony was involved in homosexuality. I can remember saying to myself, *God gave me a perfect little baby, and I turned him into a homosexual.* The sense of remorse was overwhelming.

After some ups and downs in my Christian journey, I began to seek God with a new sincerity. I grew stronger as a believer and began accepting more positions of leadership in my church. I experienced God's presence in my life in a much deeper way, and I began to accept his forgiveness for all the mistakes of my past. I could come to him with each day's problems and know that nothing could take me out of his strong hands. I found comfort in this verse (slightly adapted to fit me as a woman): "Though she stumble, she will not fall, for the LORD upholds her with his hand" (Psalm 37:24).

For many years I lived in relative freedom from guilt over Tony's continuing homosexual involvement. Then several years ago my sense of peace was shattered again. I learned that Tony had AIDS. This knowledge brought a whole new wave of guilt: "My sins not only made my son gay. Now they are killing him too."

One day I heard a word that stuck in my mind: *regret*. Somehow that one little word seemed to bring me some hope. I went to my friend Mr. Webster (the dictionary) to get a better understanding, and here's what I read: "Regret: a troubled feeling over something that one has done or left undone." I liked that definition. Yes, I could live with that! This explanation was telling me there is a sadness which comes from seeing how the wrong choices of our past can affect people we love. But that sadness isn't a sinful feeling, and it doesn't have to become our focus. With the dictionary still open on my lap, I turned to the word *guilt*: "A painful feeling of self-reproach from a belief that one has done something wrong or immoral."

In the past I had been burdened down by guilt. I knew that as a young single mother, I didn't always know what to do and I made mistakes. I wish that I could start motherhood all over again and do it right. But I can't. I regret that. In embracing regret, I choose to reject guilt.

Specific Prayers for Parents
As mentioned before, parents are especially vulnerable to guilt. But there are specific ways that we can help our children to heal and, at the same time, help ourselves move on in our lives.

Pray for strength to be open. Pray that you will have the strength to hear what your child says to you about the past. Maybe your thoughtless actions hurt her deeply. Maybe your failed marriage wounded his spirit. Be open to listen to his pain that resulted from your choices years ago. And pray that God will give your loved one the courage to talk to you about issues from the past which are still unresolved.

I was counseling with a young man one day; while we prayed, some painful memories surfaced. He stopped, looked up at me and said, "My mom is a Christian now, and she has been wonderful. But there is still some hurt over things I feel that I didn't get from her when I was growing up."

"Why don't you talk to her and tell her?" I asked.

"Oh, I could never do that. She has been so understanding lately, and I don't want to hurt her feelings."

"Michael," I told him firmly, "your mother loves you very much. I know she is praying for you. She would want you to tell her. Besides, we can pray that she will be prepared for your talk with her."

Michael and I continued praying, asking God to prepare his mother for this special conversation. Later he took a big step of faith and discussed his past hurts with his mother. The talk went well, and Michael felt a new freedom from his past.

Pray for strength to ask forgiveness. I had to be willing to go to my son and confess specific ways that the Lord showed me I had let him down. I had to tell him how sorry I was. And I have seen the powerful results of humbling myself in this way.

One day Tony was sharing with me why he was attracted to his partner, Rick (as if I needed to know!). I was surprised to hear one of the reasons: Rick had lived in the same house for many years. "I never felt stable because we moved so much when I was a kid," he explained. I had never imagined the impact of our numerous moves on him. The next day I apologized to Tony for not giving him a more stable home. He forgave me, and that night we had an honest talk about his growing-up years.

Pray for strength to endure. For many years I have been blessed to see healing occurring in the lives of many ex-gay men and women. My ministry experience gives me a better vantage point than most parents. For most of these individuals the healing process has occurred over an extended period of time. Often God has worked in such subtle ways that healing is not apparent for a long time. This process may take many years in a child's life. We have to be patient and allow the Lord to work in his timing, rather than ours.

Freedom Through God's Forgiveness

Are you weighed down with guilt? Feeling like the burden of this discovery is killing you? The psalmist David felt like that too: "My guilt has overwhelmed me like a burden too heavy to bear." He felt the same misery as you: "I am bowed down and brought very low; all day long I go about mourning" (Psalm 38:4, 6).

Does this sound familiar? If so, you can find freedom in the same way as David, by seeking God's forgiveness: "Have mercy on me, O God," he prayed, "according to your unfailing love; according to your great compassion blot out my transgressions" (Psalm 51:1).

Parents and spouses who have a relationship with God possess a great advantage over those who don't. They are recipients of God's forgiveness. That's one of the greatest gifts of being a Christian. Jesus Christ died so that we could be forgiven of our past—all of it! David had discovered this truth when he said, "Blessed is he whose transgressions are forgiven, whose sins are covered. Blessed is the man whose sin the LORD does not count against him" (Psalm 32:1-2).

When we confess our sins to him, God's forgiveness is instant. But often we have a desire to pay for our mistakes. After all, we were punished as children for wrongdoing. How can we just confess a grievous wrong and walk away totally free? We want to work at making something "right." But that is why Jesus died for us. He has already paid the price for our forgiveness, even in this specific area where we may have failed. God has forgiven us, and now we must forgive ourselves.

Forgiveness is a spiritual reality, whether or not we *feel* forgiven. Sometimes it takes our mind and emotions a long time to catch up to what has occurred in our spirit and soul. Some find it helpful to write down their confessions in a journal or make the confession to another person, such as a trusted friend, pastor or counselor.

Before Tony's announcement of homosexuality, my usual pattern of facing guilt was denial. If I had done something wrong, I would avoid the guilt feelings by escaping into television and romance novels. The idea that I could admit my guilt and receive forgiveness was foreign to me. I knew that Jesus had died so that I could be forgiven, but I had little practical application of it in my daily life.

Then came Tony's confession. I couldn't hide from the overwhelming guilt feelings anymore. I turned to God and really cried out to him. I began to see the futility of my old escapes; they just couldn't solve the problem. I could temporarily feel better (or forget about my situation) while watching TV, but as soon as the show ended, all the sadness and guilt came rushing back.

Then I read Jesus' words in John 14. He said that if I loved him, I would keep his commandments (v. 15). In the same passage he says, "If anyone loves me, he will obey my teaching. My Father will love him, and we will come to him and make our home with him" (v. 23). By this time I wanted more of Jesus in my life, and now I knew how to get it. Accepting God's forgiveness was an exercise of my faith. Jesus died to give me the gift of forgiveness.

When I began reading about the root causes of homosexuality, I felt horrible. I would cry out, asking God's forgiveness for all the things I had done wrong as a parent, then leave my prayer time feeling heavy with condemnation.

Then I read a helpful quote from Corrie ten Boom. She was discussing the verse which describes God's attitude toward our sins: "You will again have compassion on us; you will tread our sins underfoot and hurl all our iniquities into the depths of the sea" (Micah 7:19). She asked, "Where are the sins that you have confessed? What does the Bible say? Your [sin] is in the depths of the sea, forgiven and forgotten, and there is a little notice which says 'NO FISHING ALLOWED.' "[4] Corrie's conclusion: "The forgiveness of Jesus not only takes away our sins, it makes them as if they had never been."[5] I began to realize that God had done his part in extending forgiveness, but I was having a difficult time in receiving it.

I decided to have a little ceremony. During my next prayer time, I took a piece of paper and wrote down everything I had done wrong as a parent. I shed a lot of tears as I wrote these things. Then I took the note and burned it while praising God for his forgiveness toward me. After that day I had an easier time putting my past behind me. From that point on I purposed in my heart not to make that list of mistakes part of my life anymore. Now when I share my story, I concentrate on God's power to heal—not all the reasons that I have needed healing!

Other parents have gone through the same struggles, but many of them have found freedom. "I have finally experienced God's unconditional love," one mother told me. "Psalm 103:12 says, 'As far as the east is from the west, so far has he removed our transgressions from us.' This verse means to me that I can look forward to guilt-free tomorrows.

"Each day," she continued, "I put myself and my daughter in God's hands. He has set me free from my past mistakes. I can't wait to get up in the morning to see what he is going to do next!"

If we lean on God, trusting that his promises are true and that he will direct us each day, we can begin to experience the peace that we long to have in the midst of this traumatic family situation.

4

Disclosure:
Do I Dare
Tell Anyone?

*H*oward had become close friends with Jill after a short time of attending her church. He knew that he needed help with his homosexual problem and decided she might understand.

One night after church, he asked her to go for a drive. They headed for the beach, where Howard parked the car and rolled down the window. The cool breeze swept over their faces as the surf crashed in the background. Jill's mind whirled as her emotions warmed to the occasion. It had been a long time since she'd been for a drive with a man as attractive as the handsome and sensitive man sitting next to her.

Howard leaned back, closed his eyes and was quiet for a long time. Jill tried to relax, holding her breath expectantly. Suddenly he sat up and looked at her intently. "Jill, I want to tell you something about me, but you have to promise that you won't tell anyone."

Jill quickly agreed. "You know that you can trust me."

For the next half-hour Howard poured out his life history to her, ending with the events of the past two years when he had realized that he was homosexual. "I promised myself that I would never tell anyone else," he confided. "But after I fell into a relationship with the guy from my chemistry class, I knew the pressure was getting too much. I had to tell someone. And somehow I thought that you would understand."

Jill was shocked. Quickly she swallowed her disappointment and tried to offer the support that Howard obviously needed. "I'm sure that must have been very hard for you," she said soothingly. "I'm really glad that you feel able to tell me. Now I can be praying for you in this area of your life."

Later that night, Howard dropped Jill off at her house, then gave her a warm hug before she went into her apartment. Howard drove away, feeling greatly relieved. Now he had a confidante and a prayer partner. After that, Howard would always look for Jill at church and was eager to have time alone with her "just to talk."

But in the following weeks Jill felt a growing conflict inside. She tried to be honest with herself about her friendship with Howard, but it was very hard. They were just friends, right? Then why was Howard always trying to talk with her alone, spilling out the most intimate details of his life at every opportunity?

The more time they spent alone, the more Jill felt like she was involved in a romantic relationship. It felt so wonderful to have all this attention from such a friendly young man, but it also felt so wrong. Why was she feeling so confused about the growing intimacy? Where they really "just friends"? And is that what she wanted?

Finally Jill confronted him. "Howard, we can't go on like this. I can't be your exclusive friend anymore. It's too hard on me. I think you need to get counseling from one of the elders in our church."

Howard decided to take her advice. He began weekly sessions with an elder. Jill saw him less often, although they remained friends. She found that she missed the evenings out with Howard. It had been a great feeling to know how much he needed her. But in the final analysis she knew that putting a stop to their intimate talks alone was best for both of them. She had been turning the friendship into a romantic fantasy, and he needed to begin seeking significant friendships with other men to help resolve the issues underlying his homosexual feelings.

Disclosure for the Male Homosexual

Homosexual men often have a deep-seated insecurity around other males. So, often a gay man will share his secret with a woman, such as his mother, sister or a close friend.

This can be very disconcerting for the female friend, especially if she is single. Such secret knowledge about another person creates intimacy. It is easy to become overly responsible and far too involved in the situation.

"Mom, I have something to tell you. But first, I want you to promise that you won't tell anyone, especially Dad." Many sons have made this statement. Usually the mother will agree initially, then regret it later. After carrying the heavy load of secrecy for a few months, the mother will often confide in someone outside her close circle of friends, hoping that the child will not find out.

Many times the homosexual will tell one person and swear her to secrecy. Unfortunately, being "chosen" to carry this burden puts the person in a position that God never intended her to have. Suddenly she feels responsible to help this person who has trusted her with such a deep part of his life.

This confiding in one person, then swearing to secrecy, can be a big step for people struggling with homosexuality. They may feel very free after their deep secret is uncovered. But often this situation imprisons the person they took into their confidence.

Rethinking the Commitment to Silence

Usually we have promised, "I won't tell anyone" before we know what the confession is about—and before we realize how burdensome it can be to make that kind of commitment. But it is never too late to ask your homosexual relative or friend to release you from that promise, and to explain why.

One mother went back to her son after several months of carrying this secret alone. "James, your problem is now my problem. I need to talk to someone about what I am going through. I would like your permission to talk to my pastor at church. I also want to discuss this with my prayer partner."

Sometimes the person struggling with homosexuality will refuse to give permission for us to confide in someone else. At this point we must decide whether to keep bearing this burden alone or to give the person a choice: either they tell someone else or we will.

Eighteen-year-old Darren was terrified of someone in his church finding out. But finally he confided in his best friend, who kept his secret and even did some quiet research on their church's stand on the issue of homosexuality. His friend discovered that their assistant pastor had helped others with this problem.

This friend realized Darren needed some specialized help. He told Darren, "I think you should go and talk to our assistant pastor. Why don't you pray about it, and we'll discuss it again soon." After several weeks of discussion, Darren went in for some counseling and was so encouraged that he began seeking weekly help.

Often a wife becomes the confidante for the husband struggling with homosexuality. One woman felt trapped because her husband held a paid position in their church. If knowledge about his struggles leaked out, he could lose his job, their only source of income. She knew her husband needed help, but how could she dare tell anyone? She felt totally alone in this problem.

Hiding Their Homosexuality

Often parents want to protect their family's reputation. Sometimes, for example, parents hope that the child will just "snap out of it" and everything will return to normal again—soon! Why prematurely expose everything to friends and other family members?

Living with this type of secret can be devastating to a family. Usually one person at a time is told. Here is a typical scenario: The mother finds out. Suddenly she is crying all the time and can't tell anyone else why. Then there are two or three other family members holding late-night private discussions that last for hours in some remote corner of the house behind closed doors. Other family members sense the tension but don't know what on earth is happening. They might even be relieved when they too are finally told about the homosexual issue (they thought Mom and Dad were getting a divorce). Finally the last person in the immediate family is told and wonders why she was "left out" for so long.

When I first moved to Oregon, I swore my brother Dave to secrecy. My son, Tony, had already run off. Everyone had to know that something was wrong, but I couldn't face the thought of everyone knowing the exact problem. I am not sure if I was trying to protect Tony's reputation or my own (probably some of both).

One day my brother came home after playing racquetball with a mutual friend. This friend urged Dave to tell him what was wrong with Tony. Dave kept saying he had promised me that he wouldn't talk about it.

"C'mon," the friend urged, "how bad can it be? Is Tony sleeping with some old woman or something?"

As my brother told me this friend's reaction, I thought, *That's the worst thing he can think of? He would be horrified to know how bad it really is!* Of course, I had an exaggerated view of homosexuality at that time. It seemed the worst sin of all, and I didn't want anyone to know that it had touched my family.

Sometimes families have no choice in the matter of disclosure, because their child "comes out" publicly about his or her homosexuality, much to the embarrassment of the parents and other family members.

A few months ago I met a married couple at a small café. They had just found out the previous week that their nineteen-year-old daughter was involved in lesbianism. They came from a small town and took great pride in the healthy environment they had provided for their children.

The mother wept the whole time we were together. "I went to the store the other day and wore sunglasses so no one would recognize me," she explained at one point. "I was sure that everyone was looking at me."

She dabbed at her eyes, then continued. "I know there is a lot of talk about us behind our backs. We were so sure that sending our kids to a good school would keep them from anything like this."

Their daughter had become public about her homosexuality, so her parents had no choice in the matter of disclosure. This mother's pride in her family's high standards only added to her shame. In these situations the best strategy is to know ahead of time what you will say to people who ask about your child (especially if you suspect they cannot keep your response confidential). A simple reply might be "She needs your prayers" or "Like many kids her age, she is struggling with her belief system right now. Please pray for her." Then refuse to discuss the situation any further. It can be helpful to remember that there are other parents enduring similar feelings of humiliation because of their errant kids, probably many of them right in your own church.

What About Younger Children?

Many parents wonder what, if anything, to tell younger children in the home. This important decision depends on several factors:
☐ the children's ages
☐ the children's maturity levels
☐ whether the homosexual family member is still at home
☐ whether the homosexual family member is open about his/her homosexuality

The couple I just mentioned were wrestling with the decision of what to tell their fourteen-year-old son about his older sister. Because she lived at home and was rebelling in many other ways, they thought it seemed appropriate to tell their son. The daughter's behavior was affecting every part of the family's life.

When younger children see only part of a problem, they often make up their own reasons to explain the situation. With their limited knowledge they jump to wrong conclusions.

Here are common problems with the other children when a child's homosexuality becomes a focus within the family structure:

Feeling forgotten. There is a saying, "The squeaky wheel gets the grease." Too often, the well-behaved sibling is ignored during the crisis. Because this child does not know what is happening but senses his parents' withdrawal, he may turn to rebellious behavior to win the attention he craves.

Feeling jealous. Often the homosexual child is handled with special care, especially if the parents fear the child will flee the home or commit suicide. This special treatment can seem very unfair to the "good child," especially if he or she does not understand the problem.

Giving up on the family. This is the greatest harm that can come. When children stop looking to their family for a sense of belonging, they turn elsewhere. Unfortunately they usually turn to their peer group, where they can get into destructive behavior like drugs, alcohol abuse and sexual immorality.

It is difficult to know what to tell younger children. Here are some simple guidelines. First, never tell a lie. Don't give out false information, even though you may be tempted to "cover" for the homosexual child. Second, answer questions directly but simply. Don't give too much information in response to a simple question, especially from a young sibling. It is overwhelming for a child to hear more than he can process.

A younger child might ask her mother, "Why doesn't Jenny have a boyfriend? She is always hanging around the other girls." The mother can respond, "Your sister seems to like women better than men. I don't know why." This simple answer will satisfy most children.

If the child begins to ask more in-depth questions, the mother can say, "Maybe we can sit down with your father tonight and talk more about this." This response gives her time to pray and get additional support (be sure to follow up on your promise to talk later!).

My brother's children have always been very close to my son. They were very young when Tony entered into homosexuality. Though my brother has always been a big support to me, he decided to wait until his children were in their teen years before explaining Tony's situation. Because we were not living in their area at that time, it was unlikely they would find out on their own.

My brother prayed, waiting for the right time to tell each one, wanting them to maintain their love for Tony. After the disclosure, they continued to love their older cousin. They also changed their attitudes on the homosexual issue. No longer were gays just "a bunch of faggots"; now the issue involved someone they loved. They have all been very supportive toward Tony.

Bondage comes from the fear of others finding out the truth about our situation. Of course there has to be discretion, but no one should carry this burden alone.

Our Pain Helps Others

I remember when I began being more open about my son's situation. I was getting my hair cut by Dottie, a casual friend from church who was a professional stylist. The salon was empty, and I felt compelled to tell her my son was a homosexual.

However, as soon as I told her, Dottie became very uncomfortable, obviously not knowing what to say. There was a long, awkward silence. Quickly she finished up my hair and seemed relieved as I left.

As I walked to my car, I had to blink back the tears. I felt totally humiliated. *Obviously I didn't hear from the Lord on that one,* I chided myself. *That's it—I will never tell anyone again.*

The next night the telephone rang. To my surprise it was Dottie. She sobbed as she told me that when she got home the previous night, her teenage daughter told her that she was pregnant. "I knew right away that I could tell you," she said through her tears.

Because I had been so vulnerable with her, Dottie could share her deepest pain with me. It was exciting to realize that God could use me to comfort other mothers—even those without gay kids!

Another woman I know was getting ready to attend her small prayer group. This was the first time Ella had met with the group since learning her sister was a lesbian. She prayed that God would show her if she should share this situation.

Before the meeting the women were casually talking, and one of them made a little joke about "the gays." Ella realized that before this situation arose in her own family she would have joined right in the joking. Instead, she felt hurt by the remark. They were ridiculing her sister.

Soon the women were sitting in a circle, sharing what was on their hearts. When it was her turn, Ella took a deep breath and told the women about her sister.

"From that moment on, every attitude changed in our group," she told me later. "It was no longer 'them.' It was me and my sister. Those women really cared."

We can see from Ella's situation that being vulnerable can lead to much healing—for ourselves and others. If this woman had not shared with her group, she might have been hurt by their remarks over and over again. Finally, she probably would have left the group to protect herself, feeling like the wall of hurt was just too thick to penetrate. When she was vulnerable, she found the love and care that she desperately needed. Her friends learned an important lesson, but Ella was the winner too.

All of us need good friends to help us through this situation. People who know us and love us. People we can trust. Initially they will be surprised, even shocked, that this issue could arise in our family. They may say some ignorant things. But, for a moment, imagine this situation is occurring in *their* family instead of yours. Wouldn't you want to know, so you could love them and offer support? Of course! Help your friends understand how they can help you. You will all benefit as a result.

5

Relinquishment:
What Does "Letting Go"
Really Mean?

*T*he firefighter looked up as he carefully climbed the last section of the tall aerial ladder. The apartment building was rapidly being consumed by giant leaping flames. Through the smoke he could see the source of the screams above him. A woman was leaning over the railing of her small balcony. She held a small blanketed bundle in her arms.

"Hurry, hurry!" she screamed, looking down at him. "My baby, my baby!" Her figure was silhouetted by orange flames dancing behind her. The firefighter's heart pounded as he saw that the top of his ladder could not quite reach the woman's balcony. The gap stretched five or six feet. The woman realized it too, and stood paralyzed with fear. The man knew there was no time to delay. He snapped his safety harness onto the top rung of his ladder and thrust both arms up toward the woman above him.

The mother hesitated, glancing down at her infant son. She looked again over the balcony railing. The stranger was just below her, but the ground was a long way down. Could she drop her baby into his arms? What if she missed? Should she trust this unknown man's skill and experience?

The firefighter was close enough to see the fear and uncertainty in her face. He stood patiently for a few seconds, then beckoned with one hand. "C'mon," he yelled, "I'm ready." Suddenly the small bundle came plummeting toward him.

This mother's situation illustrates the dilemma of relinquishment. She knew the only way to save her tiny son was to let him go. The desperate circumstances made any other choice impossible. The child was unaware of the dire situation that forced her to make such a decision.

Most of us will never find ourselves in a blazing building, having to trust a stranger to catch our child. But there is a parallel situation in which we are involved right now: trusting our loved one into God's care. Although he is not a stranger, he does call us to let go and allow him to rescue those we love. We can destroy someone's life by holding on when we should let go.

One of the most frustrating pieces of advice, however, that one Christian can give another is "Just give your loved one up to God." It's not easy. Most people aren't sure what "giving up" really means. Are we supposed to turn our back on someone? File for divorce when a marriage situation looks hopeless? Stop challenging a child to reconsider his or her pursuit of homosexuality?

The word *relinquish* can be defined three ways:
□ to surrender a right
□ to put aside a plan
□ to loose one's hold on something or someone[1]

The kind of relinquishment we're dealing with here usually involves all three of these actions.

Who Is Affected?

All of us in some way are involved in relinquishment. We must make choices daily. Obstacles that separate us from God must be given up. We can understand this principle when it concerns material things, but when it comes to people, we may be confused about our Christian responsibility.

Also, relinquishment is difficult because it often involves someone we are closest to, the last person we would want to release.

Abraham knew the pain of relinquishment. He was a godly man who made great sacrifices for God. In response to God's command, he gave up his country, his people and his father's household to move to a foreign land (Genesis 12:1). But probably the greatest sacrifice God required of him was the voluntary relinquishment of Isaac, his only son whom he dearly loved (Genesis 22). The Lord commanded Abraham to take his son to the region of Moriah and sacrifice him there as a burnt offering. Abraham moved to obey, but at the last minute the angel of the Lord intervened so Abraham did not have to kill Isaac.

Make no doubt about it: Relinquishment can be extremely painful. It's never easy. People who say it is probably haven't yet experienced it!

Relinquishment Versus Abandonment

Relinquishment is giving someone up; abandonment is giving up on someone. There is a big difference. When we let go of our loved ones, we stop taking responsibility *for* them. But we don't stop fulfilling our responsibilities *to* them.

Parents can't save their children from all wrong actions. When our kids were little, we fixed all the hurts. When does that stop being our job? Relinquishment is a big issue for parents; it's very hard to "just let go" and trust God with our grown children.

All of us—whether we're thinking of our children or ourselves—live with the consequences of our daily choices. God is just and fair. We depend on that quality; we trust him because he is constant at all times. And he is consistent in rewarding good and punishing evil.

The Bible gives clear instructions on what will happen if we are not obedient. Look at Proverbs 1. The author, who many scholars believe is King Solomon, says that the proverbs are intended to make us wise. In verse 7, he says that the first step is trust and reverence (fear) toward the Lord.

Solomon urges us to listen to our parents. If we disobey, harsh consequences follow: calamity, distress and disaster (v. 27).

No loving parents want to see God's wrath poured out on their children. But we have a way to fight the enemy who would pull our child into deception: prayer. We can pray for our children and for wisdom to know what part we should play in their lives.

Too many parents pray only that their child will escape the severe punishment of the Lord. Instead, I have learned to pray, "God, do whatever it takes to draw my son to you." Sometimes a child's circumstances must get worse—*much* worse—before he is ready to consider changing his behavior.

God allows painful consequences to occur in a person's life as a result of rebellion. Sometimes it simply takes time until rebellious actions begin to bear bitter fruit. We must be patient, allowing that time to pass. There is little that we can do to hurry this process.

The negative results of sinful actions are one of the strongest deterrents to continued sin. So don't pray that God will remove the consequences of your child's sinful behavior—and don't thwart God's purposes by removing them yourself.

Understanding this principle helped one couple whose son was living in New York City. Their son seemed to be always "between jobs." He just couldn't stay employed, usually because of his heavy drinking and late-night partying at gay bars. He would stay out carousing half the night, then call in sick the next day. Soon his employer would catch on to this pattern and fire him.

At first this mother felt compelled to send money to help pay the rent and other necessities whenever her son called for help. But after several years of this pattern she realized that sending money was not helping her son learn responsibility, nor was it helping him face the consequences of his carefree lifestyle. Finally she and her husband agreed to stop sending money and told their son of this decision. The next time he phoned, she expressed loving concern but was firm in saying no to his plea for "a little help, just till next payday." Although her son's behavior did not change immediately, this mother knew that she had made the right decision, that she was helping her son in the long run.

Some Aspects of Relinquishment
What can we do to relinquish our loved one to God?

Face our limitations. Eventually we reach the point of acknowledging our own helplessness in relating to our gay loved one, realizing we have reached the limits of our human love and wisdom. We are ready to admit that we need to let God take over.

Nancy was sharing with a friend about Stanley, her friend who had AIDS. "When Stanley became ill, I felt that I had to be there constantly for him," she began. "He had no family, and that made the pressure all the worse." Stanley had told her of his great fear of being alone in his final days, and Nancy had reassured him that she'd always be available to help. Later, as Stanley's demands increased, Nancy felt trapped and overwhelmed. Finally, in talking about the whole situation with another friend, she gained a new perspective.

"I realized that I didn't have to do *everything* for Stanley. I began to ask God to show me my limits. In prayer, I committed to be obedient—doing only those things which he was calling me to do. I felt a huge load roll off my back. Actually, I cried in relief. And something else happened. Other friends of Stanley seemed to show up and help out after that. We became a team, a family who cared. That's exactly what Stanley needed, and God knew it." Nancy faced her own limitations—and grew in the process.

Acknowledge God's ownership. Like Abraham, we realize that the person we love belongs to God—not to us. Though we may have been entrusted with a position of care and responsibility for them, ultimately they are his responsibility.

One day I was talking with Derrick's mother about his homosexuality. "I worry about him all the time," she said, dabbing her eyes. "I can't get anything done. He's always on my mind. I love him so much."

I was tempted to say, "You need to trust God with this situation." But this response—true as it is—seemed so shallow and uncaring. Then I had an inspiration.

"Do you know that Jesus loves Derrick even more than you do?" I asked. Her look of surprise told me that the thought had never crossed her mind. "You didn't create Derrick," I continued. "God did. He used your womb and gave you stewardship of him, but Derrick belongs to him. Even though Derrick is running from God, he was created in his image. God still has a plan for your son. As you begin to understand this, you can pray for him and be better able to leave him in God's hands."

Let go of our expectations. It's natural to have expectations for those we love: hopes that our children will marry and raise families, or exciting plans for the future home and family we will enjoy after marriage. It's certainly not wrong for us to have those dreams.

But part of relinquishment is coming to terms with the fact that these things may not happen. We surrender our expectations, realizing that God will still bring fulfillment to our lives, though maybe not in the way we had planned.

Give our loved one the same freedom God gives us: responsibility for one's own choices. This is perhaps the most difficult part of relinquishment, allowing our loved ones to face the consequences of their own actions, even if they experience pain and tragedy in the process. It's important to realize that this does not reveal a lack of love on our part. God gives each of us that same freedom of choice, and his relationship to us is one of perfect love.

Give up efforts to control circumstances. In a very practical way, we begin to truly trust in the work of the Holy Spirit. Coming away from homosexuality requires a vision and determination that can only come from God. He alone can bring conviction of sin and a desire for change. We must begin to act on what we know is true: God can work out someone's situation better than anything we could come up with.

When Do We Relinquish Someone?

Though we may have friends admonishing us to "let go" of someone, God is the only one who knows when we are actually capable of doing this. Though we may be continually "giving" someone to the Lord in our prayers, a specific time will come when God will ask us to let go, and he will then provide the strength to do it.

On May 15, 1976, Barbara Johnson drove to her church for a midweek prayer meeting. It had been almost a year since her son Larry had disowned the family and disappeared into a homosexual lifestyle. She had been deeply depressed most of the past year, and today was no different.

As she drove through the suburbs of Orange County, Barbara felt the familiar burden inside. "I was tired of the churning over Larry—tired of giving him to God, and then carrying the heaviness myself. Over and over I thought I had taken my hands off and surrendered him to the Lord," says Barbara. "But I had been picking up my burden again and bringing it back home to carry around." She said out loud in the car, "God, I have had enough of this! Whether he kills himself, or if I never see him again, or if you take Larry's life, as you might do, or whatever happens—he is yours. I can't go on one more day with this overwhelming concern for him that's been consuming me for eleven months."

Knowing God had heard her decision, Barbara went into church and enjoyed the singing. Then as the pastor called for prayer for various situations, he said, "There is a mother here with a broken heart." Barbara had previously heard him say those words, and each time she knew the message was directed at her. She had even gone forward and asked for healing prayer. But today something was radically different. She sensed that the pastor was not talking about her any longer. She wanted to get up and shout, "Pastor, it's not me! It's not me!" For the first time in almost a year, his reference to a brokenhearted mother was someone else.

"I practically flew home," Barbara remembers. "My heart sang. The music just flowed out of me. The only explanation for my lightness in spirit was that I had allowed God to keep the burden of Larry. When I had finally stopped asking God, 'Why me, Lord?' and turned it around to 'Whatever, Lord,' then the burden actually lifted and I was free in my own spirit to expect God to work."[2]

What Is the Purpose of Relinquishment?

Why does God ask us to relinquish someone we love? From our finite perspective we wonder, *Could God possibly be insecure about our love for him? Why does he require such drastic proof of our commitment?*

The answers to these questions come only as we grow in the knowledge of God's character, realizing that everything he asks of us is for our benefit. The purpose of relinquishment becomes more clear as we look at the results in our lives: increased security and greater freedom.

Increased security. Relinquishment tests the foundation on which we base our lives. The Bible reminds us to set our affections on things above (Colossians 3:2), but most of us will admit our affections remain pretty earthbound.

We care deeply about our children, our families, our friends and our jobs. These are legitimate concerns. When God says he wants us to love him above all others, he isn't implying that we love others too much. He wants us, above all, to have our ultimate commitment to him and to have our ultimate security in him.

The world in which we live is unstable. The people we love are not unshakable pillars. Security in God is not an option. It is a total necessity if our lives are to be founded on something solid. If our securities have become fastened too tightly on something shakeable, relinquishment loosens our hold on the temporal and places our grasp back on the eternal.

Greater freedom. When we are able to release the one we are so concerned about to God's care, we are freed from an emotional roller coaster type of existence where our moods are dependent on our loved one's actions.

One mother of a gay son knew relinquishment had taken place when she no longer sank into depression every time her son mentioned his involvement in homosexual behavior. This is not to say that we are totally unaffected by the actions of the other person, just that we are not controlled by them.

Another benefit of relinquishment is that our minds and hearts are free to focus on other things and to care about other people. When we are so wrapped up with one individual, other relationships and responsibilities may be neglected.

Letting go enables us to engage in new pursuits with joy and enthusiasm. We are freed from the compulsion to try and bring loved ones "back to the Lord," and we are released from a sense of guilt and responsibility for their choices.

Although we may not realize it, pressure from us may actually drive someone farther from God, rather than farther from sin. Relinquishment frees us to love in a more relaxed, nonpossessive way, allowing them the freedom to choose God for themselves without the pressure of our expectations.

When a loved one has a life-threatening problem, the desire to fix the situation is natural. Often we would do *anything* to get them out of their gay or lesbian lifestyle. God appears to be moving slowly, very slowly. His perfect timing is not always what we want. We get very frustrated when we can't see what he is doing, or understand why he is taking so long.

"Lord," we pray, "I will wait patiently if only I can see what you are going to do." What are we really saying? We don't have the faith to believe that he is working all things to the good (Romans 8:28). Instead of asking him to increase our faith, we ask him to show us a peek "behind the scenes." We are not really letting go of our loved one, but still grasping for control of the situation.

This is a common struggle for spouses. *I'll do whatever it takes to make this marriage work,* a wife may think. *If he realizes how much he needs me, he won't leave. Eventually he will be so grateful for all that I have done.* Sometimes the wife goes to such extremes that she begins to remove the negative consequences of her husband's sinful behavior. He may stay out half the night, and she still will not question his flimsy excuses.

Willa Medinger went through this pattern while her husband was involved in years of homosexual promiscuity during their marriage. She finally figured out what was happening in his life, but she decided not to confront him. Instead, she began to attend a prayer group and begged the other women to intercede for her troubled marriage (although she did not disclose the exact nature of the problem).

"I began delving more deeply into the Bible and prayer," she recalls. "One day I heard the Lord say to me, 'You have to let Alan go.' It wasn't an audible voice, just a strong inner knowing. I realized that I had to stop taking care of him, stop being his mother. I had to stop building a perfect, rose-colored little world to hide the mess that our lives had become."

Willa, by an act of her will, chose to release Alan completely into God's hands—whatever happened. Five weeks later, Alan surrendered his life to Jesus Christ and, in a dramatic healing, was totally delivered of all same-sex erotic attractions. Today, over twenty years later, Willa and Alan have a strong marriage and work together at Regeneration, an ex-gay ministry in Baltimore.

Willa sees many other women struggling with these same issues. "Wives cannot stand to see their husbands suffer," she says. "I was trying to take my husband's pain away. Now I know that the Lord wanted to use the pain and suffering to bring Alan to himself. I had not entrusted Alan to God's hands. In essence, I was saying, 'God, I can take better care of him than you can.' "

Holding On to Our "Rights"

Sometimes our struggle to let go comes out in indirect ways. We seem to let go of expectations concerning our gay loved one, but we hold on by claiming our "rights" and refusing to release them to God. We struggle with many emotions—such as self-pity—when we think our rights are being violated. What exactly are these "rights" we claim and cling to?

Our right to be right. We have a strong desire for the other person to see our point of view as correct. But sometimes we can win a battle (today's argument) but lose the war (tomorrow's relationship with our loved one). God never called us to be right, but he did call us to love. People who lead a destructive life usually know that they are not making wise choices. But they have chosen to cast all care to the wind and do what feels good for the moment. Pride enters into the argument, and no one wins. Sometimes the best argument is a loving action done in silence.

Our right to be appreciated. This has been a continual struggle for me as a mother. If I act out of unselfish love, I am fine. But when I do something in order to gain recognition from my son and he fails to acknowledge my efforts, I am crushed.

When I returned to California from the Philippines, Tony was very polite, but his partner, Rick, wouldn't have anything to do with me. (Later I learned that he wouldn't see anyone due to embarrassment over his AIDS-related weight loss.) I had been preparing meals and taking them over to their apartment, only to catch a glimpse of my son as he cracked open the door to take the food!

One night before I went over, Rick talked to me on the phone and complimented my cooking. I was certain I would be invited in this time. After preparing the meal I changed from my food-spattered clothing, ran a comb through my hair and put on some lipstick. When I got to their apartment, I prayed before gently knocking on the door, my heart pounding.

Tony answered the door but didn't open it all the way. He took the food and closed the door in my face. I cried all the way home. As I prayed that night, the Lord showed me that I had all kinds of expectations attached to my "free" gift. As I repented and once again offered my gift unconditionally to the Lord, I began to feel thankful that I was able to help in this way. I had learned an important lesson—one that I have had to remember many times since then.

Our right to be treated fairly. I wish that life really *was* fair. But it's not—and I hear myself complain about once a week, "It's not fair!" Usually the complaint is expressed only to myself, and as soon as I hear how childish it sounds, I quit. But we have to face the reality that our loved one involved in homosexuality may be very self-focused right now. Self-centered people often use other people. We should not become their doormat, but we're wrong to expect that others will always respond in a kind and considerate way.

Our right to a "special" problem which no one else understands. Part of the letting-go process is releasing the "right" to have such a unique problem that no one else can relate to our pain. This is a deception that keeps us separated from others and locked into feeling sorry for ourselves. Although our exact circumstances may be unique, many others around us who have errant loved ones also know such pain.

Our right to be always happy and live "happily ever after." Many Christians seem to think that God has promised his people happiness. If we are not happy, then something is wrong. But the emotion of happiness is different from the peace that passes all understanding that God has promised us (Philippians 4:7). Such peace is illogical because it is available *during* the most difficult of times. This peace comes from knowing that God is in control and that he is able to change the circumstances.

Here's how one mother experienced God's peace in a new way: "Daily I bargained with God to take my life in exchange for my son's freedom. It seemed like all my dreams had died. Why should I even go on living?"

One day this woman sat down at the kitchen table and found her Bible lying open at Jeremiah 31. Here's what she read: "This is what the LORD says: 'Restrain your voice from weeping and your eyes from tears, for your work will be rewarded,' declares the LORD. 'They will return from the land of the enemy. So there is hope for your future,' declares the LORD. 'Your children will return to their own land' " (vv. 16-17).

"When I read this Scripture, my heart leaped with joy," she remembers. "I felt hope again for the first time in a very long time. God had comforted my heart in a direct way. I began praying with renewed faith that he would bring my son back to himself."

Letting Go of Love

Relinquishment can also be a major issue for men and women involved in romantic relationships with someone dealing with homosexuality.

DebbieLynne Simmons describes how she went through this type of crisis. A few months after she graduated from college, a young man started attending her church. DebbieLynne found him rather uninteresting until they started working on a play together and discovered a common vision for Christian theater. The two started spending a lot of time together, more time than DebbieLynne had ever spent with a man.

People began making comments about the exciting way they related to each other. DebbieLynne began praying for him and "discerning" things about his self-image. When he accepted DebbieLynne's invitation to talk about the things that God had shown her, she sensed there would soon be a dramatic change in their relationship.

"I prayed all the way over here about telling you this," he began as they got together. *This is it!* DebbieLynne thought. *Orange blossoms and wedding bells are just ahead.* Then came his announcement: "Deb, I have homosexual tendencies."

DebbieLynne comforted herself with the thought that he just didn't think he was attractive to women. Once he knew how much she loved him, he would forget all about homosexuality! "Why don't you talk to someone at our church's ex-gay ministry?" she asked him, and was stunned by his response: "I'm afraid that I'd try to seduce one of the guys."

In the following weeks DebbieLynne wrote her friend encouraging notes with comments like "Just stop thinking of yourself as gay, and those feelings will leave." But she had secret doubts. When they were out with one of his good friends, she couldn't stop wondering if he wanted to touch his buddy the way DebbieLynne wanted him to touch her. How could this godly man, who played the organ so faithfully on Sundays, feel such horrible urges?

But DebbieLynne kept loving him. "His homosexuality was my personal burden," she says now, "and protecting his secret enabled me to affirm him as no one else could. Deep down, I enjoyed the idea that he was emotionally dependent on me for his masculinity."

The idea of backing off and permitting the Lord to work was threatening, DebbieLynne admits. "If the woman leaves the healing—along with its results—completely to God, the man just might discover that he doesn't need her. And that discovery creates the danger that once he is healed, he might be attracted to other women."

Letting go feels like dying, says DebbieLynne. "For women like me who are accustomed to manipulating relationships, relinquishment is actually a death process." But submitting to God frequently requires that Christians die to their own desires (Matthew 16:24).

Finally DebbieLynne had no choice. The young man of her affections wrote her a farewell letter to end the relationship. "Suddenly, homosexuality became a formidable wall that I could never hope to penetrate," she says. She felt hopeless and began a period of grieving.

In the years since then DebbieLynne has ministered to hundreds of other friends and family members through her involvement with an ex-gay ministry. She shares a few principles with people involved in these types of romantic illusions.

DebbieLynne suggests that we follow the directive in 2 Corinthians 10:5 and make our thoughts obedient to Christ. This means laying aside our little romantic fantasies. When DebbieLynne catches herself day-dreaming in this way, she asks God to forgive her. Then she gets busy with other activities.

If our thoughts must be obedient to Christ, so must our actions. So DebbieLynne also suggests resisting the urge to create romantic situations. Men from homosexual backgrounds can feel guilty when women exert romantic expectations. Letting go of love calls us to trust God with his plans for our life. If we seek satisfaction through our own efforts, we are not trusting God and we will not receive his promise of a full life (John 10:10).

DebbieLynne concludes: "I am learning to seriously let go of my desires for marriage, while at the same time believing the assurance that God will give me the desires of my heart (Psalm 37:4)."[3]

Homosexuality is different from many other crises. Resolution doesn't come quickly; the issue may drag on for years. Friends may tire of giving you a sympathetic ear; after a few months, they quit asking for an update. They have burned out on discussing it. They are ready to tackle new problems in life.

In addition, some of us come from a codependent background that causes us to feed off the problems of others. We get emotional comfort from being needed by someone. Dianne noticed that she was always drawn to others in church who looked alone and afraid. Her gift of compassion was a wonderful trait, but sometimes she wondered if *any* of her friends were emotionally healthy.

When someone phoned with a problem, Dianne always had lots of time for them (even if she had just put dinner on the table). Did someone need a baby sitter? A last-minute substitute Sunday-school teacher? Someone to collect mail and water the plants while they were on vacation? Dianne was always available, until she got so tired that she began withdrawing from everyone—and felt an overwhelming guilt for her "failures." (If this is an issue in your life and you would like further insights, see appendix A.)

God has a plan for *your* life. He wants you to reach your potential, whether or not the other person leaves homosexuality. Eventually, you must move on and pursue other goals in life. If you want to push ahead, relinquish your loved one to God's care. It's difficult. You can't accomplish it overnight. And you may have to repeat it many times. But it is a reality you need to face. Without letting go, you will be robbed of the peace and joy that you desperately seek.

6
Sexual Abuse: Uncovering Another Family Secret

*D*ealing with homosexuality in a family member or close friend can seem overwhelming. There are so many circumstances to work through, so many questions that lack answers. After months of dealing with this issue we feel like soldiers in a war-torn zone, resting in the trenches with our weapons in hand, waiting for another attack from an unseen enemy.

For some families, the battle is not over yet. Other—even more painful—problems may be hidden under the surface, and these need exposure and healing. One of the most common is past sexual abuse in our loved one's life.

A Common Shaping Factor
Sexual abuse is one of the foremost shaping factors that result in adult lesbianism. Several Exodus leaders estimate that 80 to 90 percent of the women coming for help to ex-gay ministries have been victimized. It's also surprisingly common in gay men. One ministry leader said that half

of the men coming for help were victims of past abuse (usually by another male).

In a large majority of cases, the abuser is a male family member or trusted friend—not a stranger lurking on a dark street corner. In a few cases, the abuser is an older woman. Whatever the specifics, having one's trust violated at such a deep level causes widespread devastation that has lifelong effects.

Sexual abuse is so difficult for us to think about, especially when we also know and love the person who has been accused. Often the abuser will deny his guilt, even if the accusations are true. These situations can tear families apart, causing alienation and hard feelings that last for years. It's easy to rationalize that leaving the issue alone is the best solution. This type of thinking is common: *Everyone is already mad at Julie for her lesbian involvement. Why should I believe her claim of being abused? If I take her side, then I'll become alienated from the rest of the family too. After all, it did happen a long time ago, and everyone gets along well in the family. So why stir things up?*

The issue must be examined for one main reason: Time alone does not heal the devastating effects of sexual abuse. Every few weeks I hear a mother or close friend play down the impact of past abuse. One mother told me about the sexual fondling that her husband perpetrated on her young daughter years ago. Then she added, almost as an afterthought, "But he didn't really complete the act or anything." She implied that there was only one "really bad" form of abuse and anything less had minimal impact. Of course this was a way of minimizing her husband's responsibility. "Lesser" forms of abuse can be just as life-destroying as sexual intercourse.

In women, abuse can lead to a deep fear and even hatred of men (if the perpetrator is a male). Men are no longer "safe." The woman's deep need to connect with another individual leads her right into close relationships with other women, often women who have been wounded in similar ways. This sets the stage for lesbian bonding to occur.

In men, sexual abuse (from an older male) commonly brings great confusion about the boy's sexual identity. *Why did he find me attractive in that way?* the victim wonders. *Is there something wrong with me?* Typically, boys who are abused repeatedly experience some physical pleasure, and may seek to repeat the acts with other boys in order to duplicate the feelings of sexual pleasure and physical closeness.

When You Suspect Abuse

It is particularly difficult to confront this situation when we suspect abuse is occurring (or has occurred in the past), but we don't know for sure. Sally, a Christian mother, was involved in the lay counseling program at her church. As she began ministering to women, she became aware of several who had been abused as young girls. She began reading about sexual abuse and learned that there are common signs in young children who have been abused. These include

☐ fear of specific persons or circumstances

☐ social or emotional withdrawal

☐ fear of being alone

☐ early sexual precociousness (use of sexually explicit words and gestures inappropriate for the child's age)[1]

One night during her prayer time, Sally had a sickening realization that some of these behaviors had existed in her niece. Lynne was now a junior in college, but Sally could remember back to the family gatherings when Lynne was seven or eight years old. Several members of the family had joked about her "flirty" behavior. Sally also recalled how much specific information Lynne seemed to know about private body parts and sexual acts.

Now, thirteen years later, Sally wondered what to do. She realized that sexual abuse in Lynne's life was a real possibility. Even more disturbing, she had a feeling that the abuse had come from her brother, Lynne's father. He had been a heavy drinker during those years, a behavior pattern which eventually contributed to his divorce. Now Sally felt overwhelmed with her suspicions. The possibility of abuse seemed too hard to face. How could she help her niece without accusing her brother?

Sometimes mothers and other female relatives cannot cope with their suspicions—or even clear evidence—because of their own past abuse.

Counselor Jan Frank says, "I have worked with many women and children whose mothers, when confronted with the undeniable evidence of molestation within the family, could not face the reality and simply went into denial. I have found that frequently these mothers also were victimized as children."[2]

This statement was true in Sally's life; she had been abused as a young girl. She decided that she could do nothing in terms of directly confronting her niece, at least for now. But she resolved to stay in touch, showing love and interest in Lynne's life. She also began praying that an opportunity might arise in the future to discuss this issue with Lynne, to probe gently without naming names or suggesting directly that abuse had occurred.

Known Abuse

Sometimes inappropriate behavior is witnessed. One mother can still remember the moment when she realized something was terribly wrong in her daughter's life: "My first husband had died, leaving me a young widow with one daughter. When I remarried several years later, my worst nightmares came true. My second husband was verbally and physically abusive toward me. There was yelling, hitting, punching, slapping. It was horrible.

"My husband would take my daughter on outings, and they'd be gone for hours. At the time, I was elated. *She has a daddy who really loves her,* I thought. But our marriage continued to deteriorate.

"Then one day I was standing in the kitchen. My husband and daughter were nearby. I glanced over and was horrified to see him embracing her and giving her a passionate kiss that was only appropriate between a husband and wife. Something inside me snapped. I went crazy. I grabbed a glass bottle, broke it in half against the edge of the sink, and went after him with it. That was the day I finally filed for divorce." Years later this mother learned that her lesbian daughter—now a national leader in the gay-rights movement—had suffered years of sexual abuse at the hands of her stepfather.

Sometimes the mothers of abused daughters suspect that something is wrong but say nothing. The daughters may try to reach out for help, but their mothers either ignore or misinterpret their distress signals. Sometimes abused women know for sure that their mothers were aware of the situation but covered up for the sake of the abuser, usually a male family member.

Mothers have a difficult time facing these explosive issues. "Did your daughter ever suffer any sexual abuse as a child?" one counselor asked a mother who was seeking help for her lesbian daughter.

"Well, yes, a long time ago. My husband was a drinker . . . but that was all a long time ago, and he is a different person now."

"Did you and your daughter ever talk about it?" the counselor persisted.

The mother shook her head. "Well, no. As I said, he is a different person now, and it was a long time ago."

Whether she knew it or not, this mother was missing a prime opportunity to *really* help her daughter by acknowledging her ongoing pain from the past. She could have told her daughter, "I'm deeply grieved that you had to suffer through all that abuse from your father. And I'm very sorry that I suspected something like that was occurring but didn't confront the situation." This mother was too afraid of hurting her husband's feelings to seek true healing for her daughter.

A child who has been abused typically feels responsible. To have the behavior ignored or played down does even more damage. Although past abuse is a popular scapegoat today for all kinds of problems, as family members we have to be open to facing it as a possibility. We aren't taking sides in exposing it; we are acknowledging the abuse and its effects on the person we care about. If, in the past, we saw signs of abuse but ignored them, we are guilty of the sin of omission by not intervening. We need to face that sin, asking for God's forgiveness and confessing it to our child. By acknowledging the truth, the grown child has her or his pain validated, which is an important first step toward resolution.

Abuse and Marriage
Sometimes the horrible memories of past abuse surface for the first time

after a person marries. In the book *Haunted Marriage,* Andrés Tapia describes how his wife's past abuse began manifesting itself in their four-year-old marriage: "The fall of 1987 all our house plants died. Their shriveled-up leaves announced to the world that our marriage was drying up as well. Inexplicably, that summer, my wife had simply lost it, and I never knew what I would find when I got home from work.

"Sometimes she would be curled up in the fetal position in a corner of our Chicago apartment. Nauseous and scared, I would ask her what was wrong. No answer. Just a helpless shrug and eyes that were a window into a soul drained of hope."[3]

The Tapias' marriage went into crisis. Andrés was totally mystified by the dramatic changes in his wife. Previously, Lori had been tender, loving and full of laughter. Now her mood swings were erratic, and she gave her husband opposite messages which changed at a moment's notice: "You're too far away," "You're too clingy"; "You don't tell me what you're thinking," "You talk too much"; "Leave me alone," "Don't go away." Andrés felt dazed and confused.

It took the Tapias a year and a half to discover the root of Lori's despair: childhood sexual abuse. "As I understood later," Andrés writes, "the stability of the early years of our marriage had made her feel safe enough to trigger an emergence of painful buried memories." Lori entered psychotherapy—and seemed to get worse rather than better. Ninety percent of her symptoms matched those of people who had been sexually abused as children. As therapy progressed, the first memories were vague. But gradually they became more clear—a repeated pattern of sexual abuse on the part of someone close to the family.

At first Lori tried to deny its reality; she became even more emotionally crippled. Andrés recalls: "Every painful memory she tried to push down managed to disguise itself as something else and pop up anyway, ricocheting through the structure of our marriage and slamming into both of us." Andrés became so anxious and confused that he found himself vomiting during the day and crying himself to sleep at night. It took another four years before the emotional storm ended and the trauma surrounding Lori's abuse was resolved.

Jan Frank is another example. She describes in her book *A Door of Hope* how several years into her marriage she began to realize the impact of past sexual abuse. She and her husband, Don, had gone to bed and began caressing one another as a prelude to sexual intimacy. What happened next took them both by surprise. "All of a sudden I froze," says Jan. "My entire body became stiff as a board. I couldn't move. I felt strange. It was like I was there in bed with my husband, but I wasn't there."

Jan knew, from being in therapy about her childhood abuse, that something had triggered this flashback. She and her husband talked for a while and ruled out several possibilities. It wasn't the way he touched her; it wasn't the lighting in the room; it wasn't anything obvious. Then Jan realized what had prompted the memories of abuse at the hands of her stepfather. "The trigger suddenly became clear as I nestled to my husband's chest. He had put on the very same aftershave my stepfather had worn for years. My memory made the connection before I knew what was happening."[4]

Insights for Loved Ones

Family members can play an important role in the healing of abuse. "Warm, concerned, loving communication from family and friends is crucial to a recovering victim of sexual violence, even if she seeks professional counseling," advises Kay Scott, author of *Sexual Assault*.[5] How can we help a friend or family member who has been victimized in this way?

Provide a "safe" place to talk. An abuse victim needs emotional support from loved ones. Don't feel responsible to "fix" the problem, but become an educated friend who can provide a sympathetic listening ear. Several excellent books can help you understand the dynamics of sexual abuse and recovery (see some suggestions in appendix A).

Be prepared for some spiritual and emotional assaults as you provide support. "Hearing detailed accounts of abuse, perversion and pain can deeply wound you," warns counselor Alfred Ells in his book *Restoring Innocence*. "Make sure you are able to fully take on the other person's burdens without being overwhelmed."[6] Spend quality time in prayer, seeking God's ongoing help and direction in dealing with this situation.

Be aware of the victim's fears. Victims have many fears in opening up to someone. Here's a partial list from Kay Scott: "She may be afraid that you won't believe her, that you may tell others (police, family, friends), that you may insist she relive the attack verbally, that you will be judgmental, or that she may lose control or go to pieces in front of you."[7] Scott advises a family member or friend to talk openly about these fears with the victim.

Affirm the victim's innocence in causing the abuse. When children are sexually assaulted by an adult, it is *never* the child's fault. Sadly, however, children almost always feel they are to blame. They think, *If only I hadn't gone alone into the woods* or *It was my fault for playing outside after dark.* Victimizers are masters at manipulating the blame onto the victim, which only reinforces the sense of guilt and shame.

Watch your theology! Far too many victims have been further devastated by well-meaning Christians who have offered plastic platitudes like "It was God's will" and "God must have allowed it for a reason." Even verses meant to bring comfort (like God's promise in Hebrews 13:5, "Never will I leave you; never will I forsake you") can bring deep confusion to victims. They ask, "If God was there, why didn't he stop the abuse?" and may feel a raging anger toward the Lord. Encourage the person to ask these questions and vent the resulting emotions. Crying is an appropriate and healthy release for the inner turmoil.

Another wrong approach is encouraging the victim to "put the past behind you." This is sometimes expressed by quoting verses like Philippians 3:13-14: "Forgetting what is behind and straining toward what is ahead, I press on toward the goal to win the prize for which God has called me heavenward in Christ Jesus." As a way of dealing with deep emotional wounds, trying to forget the pain amounts to denial. Ignoring past abuse is the equivalent of putting gauze over a huge, festering wound and hoping the infection will somehow go away. The poison only multiplies.

Keep strict confidences. There is nothing more devastating to an abuse victim than having her trust violated by a friend or counselor who spreads confidential information. When Gayle began having memories of childhood abuse, she went to her pastor for support. Later, she felt devastated when she found out that he had divulged details of her confession to another person in the church whom Gayle found very untrustworthy. This betrayal only compounded her grief and sorrow over the whole situation.

There are two exceptions to this rule of confidentiality: (1) When someone's life is endangered (your friend is threatening to take his own life or another's), professional help for them should be sought immediately. (2) When someone is continuing to victimize others, your silence will contribute to ongoing devastation. Give the abuser a chance to confess to proper authorities, or take steps to reveal his behavior.[8]

A Special Word for Husbands

Building trust in your marriage takes time and consistent effort. If your wife was abused, she may have lost her ability to trust. If so, you must earn it again—one day at a time. Here's some advice from Don Frank, a husband who has been in your situation: "One of the first things you can do to build trust is to give your wife the option when it comes to lovemaking. Remember, she had no choice in being a victim. She needs to know you will still love her even if she says no."[9]

Another way, says Don, is to have times of physical affection (caressing and hugging) outside the bedroom—with no intention that this behavior will lead to sexual intimacy later in the evening. Sometimes Don will put his arms around his wife in the kitchen and whisper, "No strings attached." Other times they hold each other in bed and agree not to make love. All these behaviors in the most intimate area of marriage build a foundation of trust in your relationship.

Several husbands of abused wives mention the importance of being an active supporter of the wife's recovery process. For example, she may feel like a huge scab is being ripped off her heart each time she attends a therapy session. Things may be worse after she returns home that day. But verbalize your support and encourage her as she faces the inner pain. Ultimately, healing will come as she perseveres.

Counselors have noticed a common pattern that you should be aware of: victims attract victims. One man looked back at his serious dating relationships during college. Every one of the three women he had dated—including the woman he eventually married—was a victim of sexual abuse.

It's not unusual for a woman with a history of abuse to marry a man who also has unresolved emotional hurts from the past. Don Frank realized after his wife entered counseling how his upbringing in an alcoholic home was affecting his marriage. When a problem arises, a husband tends to blame his wife. *This is all your fault,* he thinks. *If you'd get fixed, we would be fine.*[10] It's more comfortable to shift the full blame and responsibility onto the spouse, but that leaves the husband's own issues unexamined.

Advice for Parents

If you find out that your adult child is a victim of past abuse, allow yourself to *feel* and *respond* to this devastating news. You should be appalled! You should be shocked! You might be very angry. These are appropriate reactions, and you need to move through the stages of grief for yourself. In a sense, you were violated along with your child. Your trust in that person (if the abuser is known to you) is broken.

One middle-aged woman had to face these difficult issues in her family. "Several months ago," she explained, "my sister and I were watching television and saw a report on child abuse. To my horror, she confided that our father had sexually assaulted her many years ago. Dad is still living. In fact I see him almost every week at the convalescent home where he is living. He's in his eighties and far too crippled by arthritis to do anyone continued harm. But I find that my emotions are raging like a wildfire. I can hardly stand to be in the same room with him, let alone express love and affection." This woman's reactions were normal, even healthy. Sexual abuse is a horrendous assault, and strong emotions against it are warranted.

It's healthy for your adult child to witness these emotional reactions on your part. This gives "permission" for your child to feel and respond too. Another woman, Eva, said, "My mother's younger brother abused me on several occasions. But I never said a word to anyone. I always had the idea that if I went to my mother she would play it down. I could hear her saying, 'Honey, your uncle was drunk. He didn't really mean anything.' I always imagined that I was protecting her. Now I wonder if I was just protecting myself from her inappropriate response."

Commonly, victims like Eva see themselves as unprotected by their parents during the period of abuse. *Why didn't they do something? Surely they must have known something was going on,* the victim might think. But parents may have been unaware, and discussing their perspective with the child can bring healing. They can take the opportunity to confirm their love, emphasizing that they *would* have intervened if they had known anything about the abuse.

Now Eva's mother has died, so she will probably never discover how much her mother knew about her uncle's behavior. "Our family's middle name was denial," she explained. "We were taught by example not to address uncomfortable topics in front of other people. One time I tried to broach the subject of abuse in a very general way before Mom died. But I could tell she felt very uncomfortable and didn't want to talk about it. I think being open to talking about these taboo topics is vital if you want your adult children to feel free to talk about anything that troubles them."

Finding Support
Some loved ones encourage the victim to find support and counseling but don't realize the value of seeking support for themselves. Andrés Tapia found much insight and encouragement for himself when he began meeting with other husbands whose wives were also sexual abuse survivors. "It was good to laugh with understanding at our sexual frustrations and find empathy for our confusion," he says. One night in the group, the other guys affirmed him: "We see your courage, we see your love for your wife, we see your desire to serve God." Andrés almost floated out of the room. "You might as well have told me I won the

lottery," he says. "It doesn't get any better than this."[11]

Today, by God's grace, the Tapias' marriage is strong and healthy. Lori pleads with other husbands not to give up on their wife's healing process: "We may look hard and angry and helpless on the outside, but inside most of us [abused wives] have at least one tiny place where we desperately want you to keep trying."[12]

Jack is a single man in his thirties who has also found substantial healing from his past abuse. "When I first sought counseling I had big chunks of my life that I didn't remember," he says. "I was highly promiscuous with other men and knew my life was totally out of control. I felt an explosive rage toward my family that was threatening to destroy all my relationships."

Jack had a "marginal" relationship with God, but he sought out a Christian counselor. This older man encouraged Jack to pray about his feelings, then write in a journal what he was learning. Jack was amazed at the results. "After several months, my journaling became a wonderful time of fellowship between me and God. He spoke to my heart, and I began to identify other emotions under the rage: hurt, shame and guilt. I began to write about those feelings. My sexual 'acting out' dropped quite a bit, and I didn't explode as much. It was a great day when a friend said he could see a good change in my life."

About a full year after Jack began counseling, he started to remember that he had been sexually molested as a child. In each session he could recall more and more details. "It was good to be able to identify my feelings. And by this time I had learned to trust God and his love for me. He gave me the courage to face difficult relationships within my family. I am learning how to be honest without getting angry. I have a long way to go, but now I have the tools I need to continue walking along this journey of healing."

Jack's story is a wonderful example of God's perfect timing. The Lord built a relationship of trust, then allowed the abuse memories to surface. Jack learned later that his counselor had seen signs of possible molestation early in the counseling process, but he had helped Jack develop his relationship with God first before pursuing that area of hurt. As Jack began to trust his Healer, he could face his pain and overcome it.

Don't give up. The issues surrounding abuse are complex and take much time to resolve. But with God's help, the victim of sexual abuse *can* be restored.

7

Illness:
Living in the
Shadow of AIDS

I *was serving as a missionary in Manila when I heard the news that my son* had AIDS. It was a day I'll never forget.

Tony had been living with the same man for eight years, so I was confident that he had missed being infected. Then, one day during a phone conversation, Tony mentioned that both he and Rick had the flu and were having a hard time getting well. They had decided to get tested for HIV, the virus that causes AIDS.

"That would be a good idea," I responded casually, never dreaming of the coming crisis. During a later conversation, Tony confirmed that they had both been tested and would find out the results on a certain date.

In the days that followed I seemed oblivious to any fear. Then came the big day. Tony had agreed to phone me from California after nine a.m. my time. Early that morning I went to a quiet room and stilled my heart before the Lord. Finally my fears came tumbling out of the hidden recesses of my heart. I wept and prayed.

Just after nine o'clock, the phone rang. I was in the back of the house and suddenly realized with horror that the phone was still set on the "fax" setting we used during the night hours to receive messages from our friends back in the United States. I dashed through the house, trying to catch the phone by the second ring. It was too late. As I approached the phone, a faxed message was already rolling out the top of the machine.

"You probably don't remember me," I read as the paper tumbled out, "but I am a friend of Linda's . . ." Linda was my close friend who I had lived near in Oregon. Soon I had the whole letter in my hands, and I began reading it while walking back to my room. The writer explained that she'd had a disturbing dream about me the previous night. She called my friend Linda and they prayed, then Linda gave her my fax number.

I kept reading. Suddenly one line caught my eye: "In my dream you were very distressed about your son, Tony. I woke up and felt a strong need to pray for you . . ." The letter dropped to my side as my arm went limp.

Oh, God—NO! I cried inside. In my heart I knew that Tony's phone call would bring devastating news. Just then the phone rang again.

It was Tony—and my inner conviction was confirmed. I didn't even pretend to be casual or carefree when I answered. The actual words we spoke are a blur to me. I don't think I even let Tony tell me that he was HIV-positive. We cried together as I told him that I already knew, that God had just told me. It was a precious moment between us.

When my husband, Frank, came home a while later, I told him the news: both Tony and his partner, Rick, were infected with HIV. We cried together. "It's like losing two sons," he told me. Frank said I could fly back to America to see Tony anytime. I wanted to rush over to the Manila airport, but in my spirit I sensed God saying, "No, wait. Trust me." By his grace, I was able to obey.

Tony and Rick went through many health crises in California while I prayed diligently from my overseas location. I learned a lot about waiting on God. I began to trust the Lord more deeply than ever, waiting on his perfect timing for my eventual reunion with my son.

Two years later Frank and I finished our mission assignment and returned home to San Rafael, California. Now that I was living in the same city as Tony, I began to learn many lessons about the day-to-day struggles of supporting a loved one with AIDS.

As I faced this situation in Tony's life, I asked many questions. How do I live with this killer disease? How should I respond when someone I love has an illness that, except in rare instances, leads to death? And how can I help in the best possible way?

Earlier in this book we discussed the stages of grief. Certainly the discovery of AIDS triggers another cycle. First comes the shock of the discovery, then the turbulent emotions begin surfacing. We realize it is likely we will watch this person's slow decline and eventual death. Perhaps most frightening are all the unknown crises we'll face along the way.

Many loved ones develop a thirst to know more about this foreign invader, to read books about the disease and find something to give them hope. Newspapers give news about breakthroughs in research and updates on the most effective medications. Magazines publish stories of long-term survivors. And the books! Hundreds of AIDS-related books are now pouring off the presses.

There are many issues surrounding AIDS. But in the following pages, we'll attempt to address the most common problems and questions that family members and friends confront.

What About Healing?

One of the first and most urgent questions involves the whole matter of supernatural healing. Is it God's will that our loved one is ill? Or does God desire to intervene and restore to health?

A thorough study of the Scriptures points to two contradictory conclusions, which can be expressed this way: *God is able to heal, but he does not usually intervene in a dramatic way.* The Scriptures instruct us to pray for those who are ill: "Is any one of you sick? He should call the elders of the church to pray over him and anoint him with oil in the name of the Lord. And the prayer offered in faith will make the sick person well" (James 5:14-15). This passage shows that God is able to heal supernaturally in response to believing prayer.

But other Scriptures point in another direction. In 2 Corinthians 12:7-9, the apostle Paul's repeated prayers for the removal of his "thorn in the flesh" (which many believe to be a physical affliction) went unanswered. In another instance, Paul left behind a coworker during his missionary travels because of the man's illness (2 Timothy 4:20). Some believers at Corinth were "weak and sick" and even dying because of their sin (1 Corinthians 11:30). Ultimately, all Christians—no matter how deep their faith—will die.

Here are three principles to keep in mind when wrestling with a loved one's illness.

Stay balanced. Most of us know wonderful Christian families who have lost loved ones. We may know others who have been marvelously healed. Some people make it a life goal to seek healing for their loved one. They attend every healing service in their area; they chase down every new rumor of a cure. They pursue every avenue of healing, no matter how far-fetched. For me, it's a constant battle between knowing how much to pray for healing and finding the grace to say, "Whatever, Lord!"

Pursue godly counsel. Ask God to guide you every step of the way. Talk over the options with your loved one as well as with others who can guide you: your spouse, a local pastor, an experienced doctor. Medical decisions can be extremely complex, so the input of others is helpful. Remember that the person closest to the AIDS patient is not always rational under the pressure of these challenging circumstances.

Seek the Healer, not the healing. The Scriptures urge us to pray continually (1 Thessalonians 5:17), and I pray for my son all the time. But I have less hope now for his physical healing than several years ago as I see his health slipping away day by day. At the same time, I see him growing softer toward the Lord, and I'm very excited about that answer to prayer.

Although the issue of physical healing is important, there is an even more important issue: spiritual healing. The most important kind of healing will occur when my son makes peace with his heavenly Father. Then he will go before me to a place where there is no pain, no bad days, no chance of falling into sin. His healing will be complete. I would like healing for his body. But the healing of his soul is much more important to me.

The Fight for Self-Sufficiency

As persons with AIDS slowly lose control over their lives, they fight to maintain some control as long as possible. Their reactions can be self-centered, even drastic.

Jackie knew that her brother, Art, had lost over sixty pounds and was failing rapidly, so she telephoned and said she wanted to come visit.

"Sorry, I don't want you to come," he responded. "I want you to remember me the way I used to be—not the way I am now." He assured her that he still loved her and enjoyed their chats by phone.

"But I've already bought my airline ticket," Jackie protested, expecting that he would relent.

Instead, Art became very angry and yelled at her, "I can still decide who I will see and who I won't see!"

Jackie was devastated, especially in the following weeks when her brother began refusing her phone calls. Unfortunately, Art's desire to maintain control was greater than his desire to see his sister.

Adults with AIDS want help but often resist too much mothering. As they weaken physically, they face the grim prospect of someday needing total nursing care. Family members who fuss too much may produce irritation rather than gratefulness.

Being a Help, Not a Hindrance

Here in the United States we have many support services to pursue on behalf of the person with AIDS. But with so many options the choices can be overwhelming. Many resources are available if we are willing to take the time and fill out the paperwork—for starters!

Health-care workers in the field of AIDS are often overworked and overwhelmed with the emotional toll of assisting so many desperate and dying people. We should be kind and patient—but persistent. Sometimes the best results come when we call early in the day at the beginning of the week. We can only do so much. Eventually the person with AIDS has to take over this process. It's helpful to keep a file of information about possible medical services for a later time when our loved one is ready.

When I became part of Tony and Rick's support system, I discovered they had made only small efforts to get outside help. Rick had been offended by the first social worker he met. I had no idea what services were available, but I called local health clinics and hospitals to find out. Soon I found many resources right in our area. I did all the preparatory work, filling out forms and various applications. I constantly checked with Tony to make sure that he wanted the information I was uncovering. (Rick was too weak by this time to have input.) Tony was also getting rather weak, so he was grateful for my help. Getting them plugged in to local resources was one of the most helpful things I did for them during this time.

If dementia has not impaired people's thinking, we should let them make the final decisions. They may not want certain services, and we can't force our preferences on them. They may equate accepting certain services with giving up. Our role is to assist, not run their lives.

After Rick died, I learned about the availability of free meals for AIDS patients, delivered right to a person's front door. I could see that Tony really needed this type of help. But when I suggested it, he was very opposed to the idea. Later, after his health had declined further, he asked me for the information. Now I am comforted by knowing that he can get nutritious meals whenever he needs them.

Here are a few other practical suggestions.

Learn the medical facts. Since my son has fallen ill, I've tried to study the basic medical facts about AIDS and related illnesses. I've studied appropriate medications and their side effects and have several excellent reference books on hand.[1] I watch for reports on new medications and other current developments. Sometimes Tony will phone me and ask about a new symptom he's fighting and the medication he has been given. If I don't know the answer, I know people who can help. I'm so glad to be able to help him, because there is little else that he'll let me do.

Prepare to talk about death. This can be a real challenge. "One day my husband wanted to talk about how to dispose of some of his possessions after he was gone," Wendy confessed. "I could feel myself withdrawing emotionally at his words. I squirmed and stammered, not wanting to talk about his eventual death. I could talk about it with others, but not with him. I am praying that I'll do better when the next discussion comes up." Wendy could also request some written directions from her husband so she will know what to do after his death.

It's important to discuss what kind of medical assistance someone prefers in the last days or hours. Does he wish to remain at home with his longtime lover? Seek room in a hospice? Does he want to live in his apartment until he goes into a hospital? This decision is really up to the AIDS patient. But discussing various options ahead of time can enable everyone to make appropriate preparations for the future.

Show respect toward gay friends and lovers. Some parents come into town during a medical emergency and suddenly have to face the reality of a homosexual partner's involvement with their child. Parents whose traditional moral beliefs conflict with their child's will need extra grace in this situation. It's best to anticipate problems beforehand and determine what guidelines you will follow. This might include, for example, reserving a room in a nearby hotel rather than staying with your son and his friend in their home.

The best approach is sensitive respect. Your child's partner is going through a huge crisis. If they have been together for many years, your child's death is like losing a spouse. This can be hard for us to fathom, but it is true. We can pray for the grace to offer support to both people who are suffering this together. Our actions will be remembered forever. This may be a prime opportunity for us to show Christ's love to everyone involved.

Inconsistent Moods

Persons with AIDS can be cheerful one day, then manifest a "why bother?" kind of attitude about everything the next. We may talk to them and they are feeling optimistic about the future; in our next conversation, they feel hopeless. Their health symptoms—only a minor irritation yesterday—may take on the proportion of a major crisis today. Some mood swings are due to erratic physical ailments which vary from day to day; others may be caused by dementia or the side effects of medication.

Another common manifestation of mood swings is the "being sociable/wanting to isolate" cycle. Some AIDS patients wish to be left alone on the bad days. Their desire is not a sign of rejection, so we can't take it personally. This "leave me alone" attitude can be hard, however, if we are used to being part of this person's life during the good days.

Sandy faced this situation with her nephew, Jim. They seemed to get along fine. Jim would let her help with his gardening and housework. Then suddenly his attitude would change. "Jim would shut me out of his life. I knew he wasn't feeling well, and I really wanted to help. I knew he needed me because he was sick." Sandy had to take her nephew on his terms and realize that he was not rejecting her. He just wanted to be left alone.

How can we cope with such unpredictable moods and behavior in our loved one?

Give unconditional love. Our help must be offered without conditions, expecting nothing in return. This is the ultimate act of selflessness, laying down one's life for a friend (1 John 3:16). Our heavenly Father takes delight in such service, even if we gain no earthly recognition.

Take time off. If you're with a person who requires a lot of care, try to benefit from the good days by taking a break. Renew your emotional reserves; regain God's perspective on the situation by spending time with him. We can rise above the moment, the tragic circumstances, the ongoing heartache, if our hope is in Christ. He does not take away the pain, but he helps us survive the bad days without being destroyed.

Resist false guilt. No matter how much we do, sometimes it can never seem enough. "I feel like I didn't take enough time that last year to be with Stan." Sarah's voice seemed to fade with regret as she remembered the last year of her son's life. But I had known them both; this woman took more time with her son than anyone else I had ever known. Still she was weighed down with guilt for not doing enough. We must take advantage of what we can do *today,* then resist feeling guilt over our limitations.

Pray for wisdom. Our proper role in supporting the person with AIDS may take some time to form. If we are a friend, we can seek wisdom from that person's family members. Our main role may be supporting the family, or offering assistance when the principal caregiver needs a break.

We can be alert to specific needs, then be aggressive in offering help. "Call me if I can do anything" is too vague to be really useful. It's better to make a specific offer such as, "Your laundry is piling up. Can I take these clothes home and wash them tomorrow? I'll bring them back on Thursday evening." People in crisis may not be able to communicate the specific ways that they need help.

Find supportive friends. When we are close to a person with AIDS, we suffer on the bad days with them. It's important to avoid being caught up on the same emotional roller coaster that your loved one is on, especially if you are the main helper in his or her life. Many times I felt panicky as I saw Tony's health slipping. I wanted to do something— *anything!*—to keep him healthy. By seeking God through prayer I often have found peace again. But sometimes I can't shake the fear that robs me of the Lord's comfort. At times like this I have a few friends who are "on call" at any time to help me.

One morning my emotional pain was agonizing. I had been praying for some time but couldn't find relief. I called a friend. When she answered, I could only let out a big sob. Without hearing a word, she knew who I was and what I needed. As she began to pray with me, God gave me his peace once again. For me, security comes from having true friends like her in my life.

Other Challenges

AIDS is an illness that presents many difficulties both to patients and to their loved ones. Here are three common struggles.

Maintaining personal integrity. If you want to spend time with your loved one, often it's on his or her terms. You may wonder, *Am I being honest here about my own needs and desires?* Last week, for example, Tony was having a good day and invited my husband and me over for a meal he was preparing. It really wasn't a good night for us, but I found myself enthusiastically accepting the invitation anyway. After hanging up the phone, I announced to Frank that we were going out for dinner!

At other times I've gotten up at sunrise because Tony was up and wanted to go out for breakfast with me (on a morning that I was planning to sleep in). I've seen (and paid for) a movie that I didn't want to see—because Tony wanted us to go. Like many of us, I struggle with this issue of personal integrity. I *do* say no to my son at times. But I want to spend time with Tony, and opportunities are limited. I am not always honest with him, but I am honest with the Lord in seeking wisdom. Periodically I ask my husband to help me decide if I'm getting off track. I think it's appropriate to make sacrifices in order to spend time with Tony. Prayer and accountability help me keep balanced in this regard.

Living with the unexpected. Another difficult aspect of AIDS is living on the edge of crisis. As the illness advances, a medical emergency can arise at any time.

The phone call came in the middle of the night. "Mom, I can't stop throwing up." Tony's voice over the phone sounded like the plea of a little boy. "Rick is throwing up too. I can't get up to help him." I was out of bed in a flash, still half-asleep but functioning on automatic pilot. My hands held a death grip on the steering wheel as I sped across town.

I vacillated between praying for God's help and spouting my anger at him. "This is just too much. Can't you even let us bury Rick before Tony begins getting sick?" At least in this case, my worst fears were *not* confirmed when I arrived at the apartment. Both men were not dying of some rare AIDS-related illness. They were suffering from food poisoning and soon recovered fully. I confessed my anger at God and was thankful I had been nearby to offer help.

Facing public embarrassment. There is one more aspect of AIDS that can be a tough challenge: dealing with our own inner emotional conflicts when we go out in public with our loved one after his health has deteriorated significantly.

Dorothy hadn't seen her friend Bill for several months. She knew he was very weak from AIDS, so she was excited when he answered her phone call and agreed to go with her to a popular nearby restaurant. She drove over to his apartment, then went upstairs to get him. As Bill came to the door, she hoped that her smile hid her shock at his frail appearance. His jogging suit looked like he had worn it night and day for a week. When they got into her car, his body odor was overwhelming.

As they drove away from the curb, Dorothy asked if Bill was really up to going into the restaurant. Or did he prefer take-out service? She gulped when he insisted they go in and sit in a booth near the window.

Bill not only looked frumpy and smelled foul, but he talked loudly and was demanding. He seemed oblivious to anything wrong, while Dorothy tried to hide her embarrassment. The waiters were nice, but the whole night was awkward for Dorothy. Later she realized that she had given little thought to the whole event before she called Bill. Like many other people, Dorothy was dealing with the harsh realities of having a loved one in the final stages of AIDS. It is a situation filled with many challenges.

Realizing Our Limitations
Whenever someone close has a serious illness, especially if that illness is terminal, the situation impacts all our other priorities and relationships.

Beth has two daughters living at home while they attend college. Her oldest son, Tom, recently moved back home due to AIDS-related health problems. She explains her feelings this way: "I get so frustrated at the demands of everyone else in the family. I feel like screaming at my husband and two other children, 'Don't you realize we have our whole lives ahead of us? I may have only a year left with Tom. Why can't you just leave us alone?' I know that's totally irrational, so I do what I can to spend time with him without abandoning the rest of the family."

Kathy struggled with similar issues. Her younger brother had advanced symptoms of AIDS when she flew across the country to visit him in San Francisco. Her husband couldn't understand why she insisted so strongly on spending several weeks away from her family. He had to work a demanding full-time job, then come home to two young children and a long list of household chores. After Kathy went home, she was still torn with the desire to return to the West Coast again soon, but she knew that the expenses and time away would further alienate her husband. We all have limits on what we can do and how much time we can give. Our limits depend on our personal responsibilities in other areas of our life, and how much our loved one desires our involvement.

Geographical distance is also a factor. In the final analysis, we can only do so much—especially if we are living far away. During my two years in the Philippines while my son struggled with HIV symptoms, I frequently prayed for him this way: "Lord, I am so far away and can do so little. But you are so close and can do so much."

I also prayed to release Tony. In the morning I would come to God and pour out my heart, asking the Lord to move in Tony's life and heal him. I prayed every day that Rick and Tony would not have any health problems that would make me feel torn between their needs and my ministry responsibilities in Manila. Then I would pray in this special way: "Father, you love Tony more than I do. There is nothing I can do for him today. I can't even talk to him and make sure that he is all right. But Father, you can. I pray that you will." Then I would hold up my hands. "Take Tony today and watch over him. I leave him in your capable hands. Help me to leave him there for this day. Give me a peaceful mind so that I can be about your work."

After this prayer, I didn't talk about Tony, think about him or even pray for him during the rest of the workday. I could trust that God was watching over him, and I resisted becoming obsessed with worry. I was also comforted by such Scriptures as "Don't be weary in prayer; keep at it; watch for God's answers and remember to be thankful when they come" (Colossians 4:2 LB).

The Question of Salvation
"But my loved one is not a Christian," some people protest. "How can

I find peace in this situation?" What they are really asking is, "How can I get him right with God before he dies?" There are no easy answers to this dilemma. I am unsure of the eternal destiny of some of my loved ones who have died. But in one way, being unsure *is* my comfort. I am not their judge. I do not know what transpired between them and God in their final hours.

Many people are demonstrating God's love to my son every day. Others are praying for him. I know the Lord is wooing him in a multitude of unseen ways. Tony does not talk with me about his spiritual condition, but I know that God is at work. If AIDS has its way and I watch my son die, Jesus will be right there with us—whether or not we sense his presence in some dramatic way. Tony's spiritual choices are his, and his alone.

Do I struggle with this whole situation? Yes! One day I am calm and trusting God. Then comes a small change in circumstances, and my peaceful world blows apart. Two main things throw me into a state of anxiety: Tony does or says something that makes me realize he is not as open to God as I had hoped, or some physical sign shows that his health is slipping and his remaining time is shorter than I had thought.

These things throw me off-balance emotionally. I have to regain my peace through prayer, sometimes calling a close friend to pray with me about this whole situation. One day Tony came back from the doctor with a gloomy report. I prayed for a long time, but couldn't fight off the inner panic. My husband, Frank, was not available, so I called my brother. He prayed with me, then added, "Anita, don't look at the water. If you do, you will sink." He was referring to Peter's attempt to walk on the stormy sea to Jesus (Matthew 14:30). When Peter saw the wind and waves, instead of fixing his gaze on the Savior he began to sink. Peter's words were the cry of my heart: "Lord, save me!" My brother's exhortation reminded me to keep my eyes on Jesus, not on my circumstances. His words really helped me, and I think of them often.

Suicide
People with AIDS may struggle with thoughts of suicide. Several factors

push them in this direction. They have cycles of good and bad days. When their health is bad, the negative thoughts increase. They also have many fears connected with a lingering illness. *How bad will it be at the end? Will I be in terrible pain?* They also have the fear of giving up control of their own life. Some days it seems easier to take a "short cut" by bringing on death quickly. Committing suicide gives the appearance of regaining control.

A mother who is a dear friend shares this incident out of her recent experience: "A few days after my son's partner died, I felt very weary. I had just found out that my son, Ed, had hidden his partner's unused pain medication. Now Ed had enough drugs to kill himself—and he admitted that's exactly why he hid the drugs. I believe suicide is wrong, and I hated living with the fear that my own son would decide at any time that his 'quality of life' had slipped below some unknown indicator, prompting him to take the morphine and quietly slip away.

"On the other hand, I had seen his partner die—and his death had been worse than I anticipated. Ed had also seen it. How could I demand that he go through the same thing? And how could *I* face it again, this time with my own son? The thoughts crushed me. But as I pondered the whole situation, I realized that God had poured his grace down on me as I sat with Ed's partner during his final days. I had divine strength for those difficult days and nights. And I knew that God would also give me the strength if I had to face Ed's death in a similar way. The Lord had been faithful to me in the past; he would be faithful in the uncertain moments of the future."

Should we discuss suicide with our loved one? I don't know. We certainly need God's wisdom and sensitivity in considering this question. This friend of mine, on a day when her son was feeling better, decided to bring up the topic of suicide as they sat at an outdoor café. "Ed," she began, "I really want to be part of your life when you are sick."

"Don't take it personally," he responded, "but I don't like anyone around when I'm sick."

She boldly pressed on. "But you are going to be sick a lot."

"I'm not planning on it." This mother was devastated by her son's response. The silence grew between them, and suddenly she had no desire to continue the conversation. Her son had previously mentioned his intention to commit suicide as the end drew near. Along the way, she hoped that he had changed his mind. Was she just caught up in wishful thinking?

"As I drove home that day," she told me, "I continued to struggle with the implications of Ed's words. Once again, I was not in control. The Lord knew exactly how many days Ed would remain on this earth. That's his promise in Psalm 31:15. I couldn't decide for Ed whether or not he would take an active part in ending his life. But I could pray that God would give him a desire to live, not die. And desire not only physical life, but eternal life as well."

Benefits from AIDS

Although it might be hard to believe, there can even be some changes for the good that come out of this difficult situation. I have experienced at least three.

Increased family unity. Sometimes tragedy reunites families who have become estranged. Children become honest with parents about their struggles. Parents thereby gain new opportunities to share their love and concern.

Faced with the brevity of life, families may develop a deeper appreciation for each other. They become less demanding. The person with AIDS may need help in all kinds of ways. Family members draw close in order to offer support to him and to each other. Many men move home for their final months of life. It's a time to make peace.

My son became involved with Rick, fifteen years his senior, shortly after Frank and I married in 1984. My husband and Tony were beginning to develop a father-son relationship, then Rick came along and stole the fatherly role. Years later, when Rick died, Tony was left alone. So Frank was able to step back into his former role, meeting Tony's need for a father. We are enjoying being a family once again.

Renewed passion for God. While I was in the Philippines, I desperately asked God to care for Tony while I was away. My long pleading hours in prayer gave me a peace that would last most of the day. It wasn't long until I was seeking God, not only for Tony, but also because I had a deep desire to know him better. Through this process, I fell in love with the Lord all over again, just as I had when I was a new believer.

When I returned to the United States, I was excited to hear on the radio a sermon by Charles Stanley called "A Passion for God." Immediately I sent away for the four-tape series. Stanley, a Bible teacher and pastor of First Baptist Church in Atlanta, helped me put into words what I had been experiencing. He challenged me in cultivating a passion to obey God, to serve him and to proclaim him to others. I had been embarrassed to think of my love for God as *passion*, as the word seems linked to sensuality. But Stanley defined passion as "an overwhelming intense desire towards something or someone else. Passion is not limited to sensual or sexual feeling but can also be directed to something that is spiritual."[2] God had given me a renewed desire for himself through dealing with Tony's situation. I am thankful for my desperation which led to this deeper relationship with God.

Fresh priorities. Time with my son has become a high priority in my life. Last Saturday night the phone rang. "Mom, do you want to go with me to the Farmers Market tomorrow morning?" Local farmers in our area bring their fresh produce every week and set up stands in a huge parking lot behind city hall. It's a popular event, and I knew it would be a fun outing.

"Sure," I responded. "But I have to go early because I have church before lunch." Early the next morning, I was standing across the aisle from Tony, sipping my coffee while he looked through the fresh tomatoes. My eyes searched his face, noting with satisfaction how healthy he looked. I didn't need any vegetables, so I just watched him shop. His handsome face was serious as he studied the produce; then he looked so excited as he found just what he wanted. Everything seemed so . . . normal, so happy.

Then the fantasy burst. Tony turned to me, and there was pain in his eyes. "Mom, I need to go home now. I'm tired." I didn't bring home any purchases that day, just some memories that I will always treasure in my heart.

When the Shadow Lengthens

The time comes when we see disheartening physical changes in our loved one: skin problems, foul breath, weight loss. We see young men age quickly. We begin to live under the shadow of death.

Living with AIDS means living with sorrow. Some have suggested that I step away from all public ministry while Tony is ill. There is some wisdom in that suggestion. What if I was scheduled to fly across the country for a seminar and my son's health hit a major crisis?

All things considered, though, I have decided to carry on. God has called me to this ministry, and he has used my testimony to help others. He has given me the strength to persevere, so I have chosen to continue ministering.

My grieving has not ended; my burden has not been taken away. I face sorrow ahead, but I know my situation is not unique. Many others carry a similar burden, even if their loved one is not infected with AIDS. There are hundreds of other tragedies with different circumstances but the same devastating impact on loved ones. I have a message of hope to give others, something that brings redemption out of the death and sorrow in which I live.

I've also realized that it is all right to live with conflicting emotions. God is helping me to sort through them. I compare my situation to a pie that contains a mixture of bitter rhubarb and sweet strawberries. Taken separately, they taste very different. But blended together and cooked in the heat of the oven, they bring nourishment and delightful refreshment to everyone who partakes of them.

So it is with my life and Tony's AIDS. There is a mixture of joy and pain, sorrow and hope. The pressures of my life circumstances feel like a hot oven, but I trust that through the lessons I am learning, others will find spiritual nourishment. I will be able to comfort others with the same comfort that God is giving me through this difficult time (2 Corinthians 1:4).

Facing the End

"Our family was gathered in Brian's room, and we knew the end was near." Maria, whose son had recently died of AIDS, was visiting to tell me about Brian's final moments on earth. "I didn't want to turn him loose, but I knew he was ready. He began to have trouble breathing and was pulling off his oxygen mask with his hand. I panicked and yelled for someone to get the nurse as I fought to get it back on.

"I thought he was delirious and unaware of what he was doing," she continued. "Then Brian opened his eyes and said, 'Mom, I see Jesus. It's time to go.' "

Maria was quiet as she wiped away a tear. "He had such peace on his face. I knew it was time. The nurse rushed in and tried to put the mask back on his face. But I stopped her. At first the nurse thought we were all crazy. But then this presence filled the room. We all felt it, even the nurse. It was a sense of overwhelming peace. That's the way our son died."

I had known Brian for five years before his death. Even though he slipped away peacefully, he was very sick in the last months as his illness progressed. Brian had rededicated his life to Christ at the beginning of his illness, and he lived for the Lord throughout his battle with HIV disease.

I have heard many encouraging testimonies of men returning to their spiritual roots, having a wonderful reunion with their family and seeing God glorified—even in their dying moments. Not every family's situation is so positive. Some men suffer dementia and become very unpleasant in their last days. Does this mean that God has abandoned them? Not at all. It just means that the illness affects everyone differently. Many things about death and dying we simply cannot understand.

"Most of us are quite afraid of dying," says author Henri Nouwen. "The slow deterioration of mind and body, the pain of a growing cancer, the ravaging effects of AIDS, becoming a burden to your friends, losing control of your movements, being talked about or spoken to with half truths, forgetting recent events and names of visitors."[3] All these fears and many others face every person with HIV.

Nouwen is a minister who has helped numerous AIDS patients face death. He has been at their side as they were ushered into eternity after being debilitated by HIV. While reading his book *Who We Are,* I was comforted by a beautiful analogy. He likened the pain of death to a mother's labor pains in giving birth. From our earthly viewpoint we see death as the end; but from eternity's perspective, a new life is beginning. "We leave the womb of this world and are born to the fullness of children of God," he says. What a wonderful way to describe such a difficult transition!

One man dying of HIV, in facing his own transition out of this world, expressed the same idea in different terms. "I can face death now without fear," he said, rejoicing that he had recommitted his life to Christ when he came down with AIDS. "I'm so grateful for these last four years of walking closer with God. Even if I'd repented on my deathbed, I wouldn't have had this chance to know God the way I have, to see how wonderful he really is."

This man knew his time on this earth was short, but he added with confidence, "My relationship with Christ is a gift beyond measure, and I'll have it with me for all eternity. Not even AIDS can change that."[4]

8
Just for Parents: Special Concerns & Questions

A *child's confession of homosexual involvement hits parents hard. This* chapter is primarily geared to help them, but much of the material covered will also help other family members, such as stepparents, grandparents and siblings.

Distinguishing Acceptance from Approval

Christian parents struggle with knowing exactly how to treat their gay child. Usually they want to continue showing love, but they worry about appearing to approve of the child's homosexual behavior. Some parents feel they need to withhold acceptance because they equate it with approval. But the two words mean different things. What's the distinction? *Acceptance* means "acknowledging what is true." It recognizes the reality of a person's choices and behavior. *Approval*, on the other hand, means "affirming something as good or right." It validates a person's choices and behavior.

All grown children make choices with which their parents disagree. A parent does not—or should not—actively intervene at every chance to show disapproval.

It's appropriate for you to let your rebellious children know that you hurt for them. Let them know why you think their choices are unhealthy. Let them know that you will always continue to love them. And let them know that you will be praying for them. After clearly stating your position it's time to back off and simply love them. From then on, they will know your stand on their actions.

Soon after I found out about Tony's homosexuality, I was reading some literature from a national pro-gay parents' organization. One article said that "fundamentalist Christian" parents were the worst kind of all for their homosexual children. I was devastated—I even (briefly) considered forsaking my conservative faith in order to help my son. The thought was rather irrational, but that's how desperately I wanted to help Tony through his crisis.

But as I reevaluated the basis for my convictions on this issue, I knew that I could not change my opinion. Did I believe the Bible was true? Yes. I could not leave the truth and follow a lie for anyone, even my wonderful son. Tony was resisting the truth, not me.

My responsibility was to love him, giving a love so deep that it was unaffected by his actions. His resistance to God's truth was ultimately an issue between him and God. His rebellion was primarily hurting him, not me.

Always separate a child's personhood from his or her behavior. Some grown children push aggressively for acceptance of their immorality. "If you reject my homosexuality, you're rejecting me." This attitude is based on their inability (or unwillingness) to distinguish between *who* they are and *what* they do.

As a parent, you know better! How many times during your children's early years did you correct their wrong behavior? Did you stop loving them? No. Remind your adult son or daughter of this difference that you have demonstrated all of their life. You are being consistent now in rejecting their sexual practices while still loving them as an individual.

Persist in what you know is true. Denying the truth doesn't change the truth. Throw back the challenge to them: Are they willing to continue accepting you, in spite of your beliefs against homosexuality?

What About Visits?

Knowing how to handle visits—either when you visit your child or when he or she visits you—can ease the situation. You might make both yourself and your child more comfortable if you try a few practical suggestions.

Plan ahead. Think through the situation, and plan according to your convictions. Some parents walk into awkward situations without thinking first and then feel too overwhelmed to make clear-headed decisions.

One mother called me to ask advice about visiting her son and his partner in San Francisco. "I don't know if I'll feel comfortable in their home," she said. As we talked, my mind jumped back to the first time I saw the unmade double bed at Tony's apartment. My stomach had tightened at the sight.

As this mother and I talked, she decided to stay at a motel, despite the extra expense. Planning ahead did not eliminate all the difficulties of the upcoming visit, but it did take care of some major decisions that faced her.

Take homosexuality out of the picture. For help in deciding how to handle a particular situation, pretend for a minute that your son or daughter is inappropriately involved with an opposite-sex friend. How would you handle *that* situation? Now apply those same principles to your child's gay partner.

Wendy was in turmoil. Her lesbian daughter was coming home to visit and had announced that she was bringing her "friend" as well. Wendy and her daughter had just started to mend their relationship after years of antagonism. Now Wendy felt her daughter was testing her. She went to her pastor for some help.

"How would you handle this if your daughter was bringing home a live-in boyfriend?" Wendy's pastor asked. "Would you allow both of them to come?"

Wendy thought for a minute. "Yes. I'd welcome them both into my home. But I would insist that one of them sleep on the couch and one in the guest bedroom." Suddenly she grinned, realizing the answer to her dilemma.

Later, Wendy phoned her daughter and explained her position. "You're welcome to bring your friend," she said, "but I want you to sleep separately. I would ask that of any unmarried couple staying overnight here." When her daughter realized that Wendy was treating her just as she would any heterosexual couple, she agreed. The weekend visit was a positive one.

Some parents fall into a double standard. They minimize the problem when their son at college is spending nights at his girlfriend's apartment, then have a fit when their daughter is sleeping with another woman. Yes, it's common to wish that our child was falling into "normal" sexual sin. But God looks at all sex outside of marriage as displeasing to him and damaging to the persons involved.

Seek counsel from parents in a parallel situation. Perhaps you don't know other parents with a gay child. But you may know several couples dealing with children in other forms of rebellion. Seek their insights; you will be amazed at how relevant their wisdom is to your situation.

"One day I talked about my lesbian daughter with another mother at church," said one woman. "It was amazing how well we could understand and help each other. Although her son wasn't gay, he was rebelling by pursuing the wrong types of friends, and she was really upset with him. Our situation, although somewhat different, had so many parallels that we have been talking regularly about our children ever since."

Dealing with Your Child's Partner

One of the most difficult issues regarding your child's homosexuality involves knowing how to deal with sexual partners. Should we shun them? Welcome them into our home? Invite them for dinner on special holidays? Parents deal with a lot of confusion in sorting through these questions.

When my son Tony settled down with his full-time partner, Rick, I was filled with mixed emotions. I didn't like the way Rick related to my son. He wasn't kind and seemed to treat him like a little boy. But I was most bothered by the fact that he interfered with our mother-son relationship. He teased Tony about any time he spent with me. Often he made me uncomfortable by repeating something personal that Tony had confided in him about me.

On the other hand, I felt relieved in some ways. Tony seemed more content. He was no longer "out on the prowl" in homosexual bars or dangerous gay areas of nearby cities. With a steady partner, his risk of AIDS infection seemed lower. I was more grieved by Tony's lack of interest in spiritual things than his day-to-day situation with Rick. Besides, I felt powerless to *do* anything about the relationship.

I struggled with a proper response to them as a "couple." As a Christian, I didn't want to validate their relationship. But at the same time I didn't want to anger Tony or alienate Rick. Certainly it seemed biblical to show love to both of them. But accept them as a couple? No way!

Major holidays usually bring this issue rushing to the surface. Your child is coming home for Christmas—but doesn't want to come alone. How should you react? What do you say? There are no easy answers.

I remember looking for an appropriate gift the first Christmas after Tony and Rick entered into a committed relationship. I was trying to find something nice, but an item that was not a "couple" gift. It was frustrating, to say the least. How could I show love without approval? In the years since that Christmas, I've gained a helpful insight: *Your child's partner is not the enemy.* He or she is someone God loves—just as he loves your son or daughter. Jesus died for the redemption of both of them. Maybe your child's "significant other" has a parent, aunt or grandmother praying for his or her salvation. Or you might be the only view of Christianity this person ever sees. You can be an important influence on their eternal destiny.

It's not uncommon for your child's friends to have some church attendance in their background, as Darren's mother discovered one Saturday afternoon. Darren's homosexual partner, Mark, stayed in the car (as usual) while Darren went into his parents' house to get some winter clothes stored in the attic. Soon Darren came back out, announcing, "Mark, my mother wants you to come inside."

As Mark walked in the front door, he heard the tune of a familiar song. Darren's mother was playing an old hymn on the piano, and soon Mark found himself humming along. In the following months, Mark visited many times, even joining some hymn sings around the piano with Darren's family. In time, Mark renewed his commitment to Christ and left homosexuality.

"I always resented Mark," Darren's mother confessed later. "But that day I saw him sitting out in the car and felt the Lord prompting me to invite him into the house." She had no idea of the profound impact that her kindness would have on the future course of Mark's life.

Mothers and Sons

Many mothers have a very close relationship with their homosexual son. Sometimes the relationship is so close that it becomes unhealthy, even bordering on a state of "emotional adultery." Typically, the son is his mother's confidant. She talks about her marital problems with him, rather than working them out with her husband. She looks to the son for emotional support and comfort when things go wrong.

In some cases, the mother's behavior crosses the line into sensuality. One man told us that, as he grew older, his mother began to comment on the size of his genitals—something entirely out of character for her. This behavior continued until he insisted that she stop discussing such a personal issue with him.

Single mothers and women with abusive or emotionally distant husbands are particularly vulnerable to becoming overly dependent on their son.

I raised Tony as a single mother and married my husband, Frank, when my son was twenty years old. Tony and I are very close; I try to be constantly aware of getting overly involved in his life, but I haven't always been successful. I remember one time in particular after my mother's death in 1989. I was grieving her loss; at the same time, I was preparing to leave for Manila on a three-year missions assignment. Even though Tony lived five hundred miles away, we were constantly talking on the phone. After all, I reasoned, Mom had been an important person in both of our lives, and we shared a deep sense of loss. I allowed myself the luxury of constant contact with my son because soon I would be living on the other side of the world.

Several years later it happened again. Tony's homosexual partner of ten years died of AIDS-related illness. I knew that Tony's life would probably also be shortened by HIV disease. Once again I began struggling to find the balance in relating to my son. I knew that he could be gone within a relatively short time span. So I sought to enjoy our relationship without being too consumed by his problems. But I wasn't always successful.

Even today, accountability with my husband and friends helps me in the daily decision to stay focused on God and the other responsibilities he has given me. But one thought is never far from my mind: *Call Tony and see how he is doing.* Overall I think our relationship is balanced, but I know this is one of my weak areas.

How do we know when the parent-child relationship is *too* close? In general, there's a problem when we manipulate circumstances to meet our relational needs. The relationship becomes emotionally dependent, a subject discussed by Lori Rentzel in her helpful booklet *Emotional Dependency.*[1]

Lori mentions several signs that can signal an unhealthy dependency by a mother toward her son.

Feeling overly responsible for our son's behavior or emotions. When we take on another adult's problems as our own, we are getting overly involved.

"What do you mean, you're not going?" I almost yelled at Tony one day. He had just informed me that he had—once again—canceled an arranged trip to my brother's house. I felt so embarrassed. How could he do this to his uncle one more time? Later, after I calmed down, I learned that the repeated cancellations were no big deal to my brother. And, once again, I reminded myself that Tony was an adult who was fully responsible for his own decisions.

Being unwilling to make short- or long-term goals without checking with our son. This is a sure sign that our relationship is overly dependent. Seeking preapproval of our plans with a spouse is appropriate, but not with a grown child.

Becoming angry or upset when our son withdraws, even slightly. If our child is not available on a certain day, this should not ruin our whole day. When we feel down because our son is not free or doesn't want to see us, this indicates an inappropriate response.

Having a constant need for our son's approval. Many people with low self-esteem feed off the approval of others. This dynamic can be destructive. Some parents, for instance, have compromised their moral convictions about homosexuality in order to retain their son's favor.

Feeling the need to control our son and his circumstances. When our children are young, we are used to being in control. There is a point, however, where we need to let go and give up tight control. This becomes more difficult if a son's health is declining due to AIDS. Still, we must allow our child to make the key decisions about his health care without manipulation on our part.

Being a compulsive helper. Some people are gifted problem-solvers and enjoy being on hand to help others. Most mothers are naturally that way with their children, no matter how old their "kids" are! But many mothers hinder God's work when they get into "overhelping." Like Mary. When her son who battles homosexuality would share his latest struggle, Mary found it hard "just" to pray for him. She wanted to drive over to his apartment immediately to see how she could help.

Mary admitted, "I would find myself in the car, driving over to his place and praying on the way, 'Lord, how can I fix this situation?' Later I realized that often my son didn't even want me to do anything—except listen to his frustrations and support him in his struggles." Mary says that she tries to sit still and pray before leaping into action. "Sometimes I sense that I'm just to pray; the Lord is trying to get my son's attention. Other times, I can help in some small way. I get a clearer sense of my part if first I wait on God for direction."

Manipulating circumstances in order to build our son's dependency on us. Sometimes we need to examine the underlying motives of our behavior.

Sharon resisted helping her son pay to get his car fixed. "I don't want him expecting me to bail him out all the time financially," she told a counselor. She wasn't expecting the counselor's response: "But with his car not running, doesn't that make him even more dependent on you?" Sharon knew that her son was constantly calling for rides. She had to admit that she was rather glad his car was broken. It had given her much more time with him, and she had really enjoyed their discussions. But now, she realized, it was more appropriate for her to give him the small amount necessary to get his car repaired.

Being the "bridge of communication" between our son and his father. A mother who takes this role may feel that she is doing a great service to benefit her son, but in truth she is often doing more harm than good. This is true for three reasons. (1) She is preventing her son from establishing an emotional bond with his father, which is exactly what he needs to do. The son fears drawing close to his father, so the mother steps in to protect her son. But she succeeds only in reinforcing a negative view of his father. In effect, she is saying that the father is likely to be harsh and unloving and that she is the good parent who loves and understands him. (2) She is acting as her son's defender and protector, and this only increases his inappropriate need and dependency on her. (3) She is feeding her own need to be in control. Being the go-between is a position of great control and importance. Instead, she must abandon her authoritative role and encourage the father to communicate directly with his son. As she trusts God to direct her husband, she will be contributing to a healthier family dynamic.

Why Does It Matter?

Maybe some of the above symptoms describe the way you relate to your son. Why does it matter that we focus too much on our son? And why should we make an effort to bring balance into this relationship?

It can be unhealthy for the other person. Male homosexuality is rooted in a lack of male affirmation. A woman is not able to rectify that need. And crowding out other relationships in our son's life can prevent him from attaining healthy relationships with other men so that his need for appropriate male bonding can be met.

It tends to destroy other relationships. When we are preoccupied with one relationship, we neglect other primary relationships. This can cause problems with the other important people in our life, especially our spouse, children and our own parents. Every other relationship suffers at the expense of this one.

It can be spiritually unhealthy for us. Obsession with a relationship can become idolatry. We concentrate on the other person rather than focusing on God to meet our needs. Ultimately we may even drive our son away from us because we are "smothering" him instead of being a healthy influence.

Finding Solutions

What steps can we take to bring balance into a "too-close" relationship with our son?

Seek different activities. We can develop interests that don't include the other person, but that are still enjoyable to pursue. This step may take some time, effort and prayer.

Get a support system. Too frequently we try to solve our problems on our own. It helps greatly to have a few trusted friends with whom we can be accountable, even if it's through a five-minute phone call on a regular basis. If you are married, discuss this issue with your spouse and ask for help in being accountable.

Commit the issue to prayer. Each morning, commit this relationship to the Lord. Ask his help in making healthy choices that day. Ask God for his wisdom, and commit yourself to one step at a time. "Today, Lord, I am going for a quiet walk alone because I desperately need a break. I won't change my mind, even if my son calls and wants me to do something with him." Seeking increased intimacy with God will help you become less dependent on the people around you.

Work on other friendships. A consuming relationship crowds out other important friendships. Developing other friendships and investing in them will be an immense help in breaking the cycle of dependency.

Be willing to examine old patterns and seek new responses. How have you made your son dependent on you in the past? What could be a first step in decreasing that dependency? You have spent a lifetime learning these relationship patterns. It may take a long time to learn new habits. Be honest with yourself and others. Take a small step every day to change. Things will improve slowly as you build a healthier relationship with your son.

Fathers and Sons

One woman was talking to her husband about her concerns with their gay son. They had found out about twenty-two-year-old David's sexual involvement a few months ago, and both of them had been perplexed ever since on how best to respond to their son's lifestyle.

When she brought up the subject of David's possible infection with AIDS, her husband exploded. "We've already gone over this a hundred times!" he yelled. "I've dealt with it. I want to move on. Why can't you?" Some Christian husbands even mask their reaction behind a spiritual façade: "I've given it to the Lord. Why can't you?" This reaction, of course, makes the wife feel totally unspiritual and quickly brings any productive discussion to an end. Another husband retorted, "Aw, it's just a phase. All guys go through that experimentation stuff—he'll grow out of it." Minimizing the enormity of the problem is another form of denial.

Too many men are experts at "stuffing" their feelings. They are able to bury some very difficult things deep inside. A homosexual son can cause tremendous turmoil in his father. In some fathers' eyes, this situation reflects on their own masculinity—or lack of it. Some men punish themselves with derogatory thoughts like *How can I be a real man if my son is queer?* The whole situation seems so foreign, so overwhelming.

"I was totally devastated when I found out about my son," admits Tom Taylor of Philadelphia. "I felt no anger. I was just wiped out, thoroughly flattened. And I felt great revulsion over the physical aspects of Peter's sexual life." In the following months, Tom struggled with thoughts like *What would people say about me as a father if they knew about Peter's homosexuality?* At that point, Tom felt convicted that he was more worried about his own reputation than about loving his son. It took a full three years before Tom had a major breakthrough. "While on vacation with my family in the summer of 1988, I found my heart was changing and I could begin to really love Peter as my son in a far deeper way than I ever had before. I was also able to show love to his partner."[2]

For some fathers, the whole subject brings up strong negative feelings for reasons that others wouldn't suspect. "The grief and pain were strong," says one father, "but I also had another reaction: deep sadness. Unknown to my son, I had been molested by a homosexual man in New York City when I was about fifteen years old. Then, in my thirties, a friend who was the associate pastor of a nearby church committed suicide when his wife left him for another woman. This was an emotionally loaded issue for me."

A great majority of gay sons feel a lack of bonding with their fathers. This realization can make a father feel guilty, whether or not this characterizes the relationship with his own son. But even the weakest relationships can be strengthened. It's never too late to spend time together.

Many fathers, realizing the importance of physical affirmation, make an effort to show a deeper level of affection for their son. "Hugging still isn't an easy thing for me," admits one older man, "but the Lord showed me that fathers and sons need to show that kind of affirmation. I never hugged my son, and he looked for that approval later on through homosexual relationships."

Many older men never saw a model of affection or good communication from their own fathers, so they struggle to demonstrate these traits to their sons. Finding other men who model these qualities can be helpful. Tackle these issues one small step at a time. A whole lifetime of learning can't be undone immediately. For example, fathers who are uncomfortable with physical affection should realize that a full embrace isn't necessarily the first step. A hand on their son's shoulder or a quick sideways squeeze with an arm around their son's shoulder can be the icebreaker in providing the physical affection that a son so badly needs. Some fathers think that being too affectionate with their sons will turn them into homosexuals. Actually the exact opposite is true: young boys who are liberally affirmed by their fathers will be less likely to look for that affirmation in the arms of other men when they are older.

Fathers who live a great distance from their sons can bridge the miles with a phone call or quick note. Most men leave the letter writing to their wives, but even a small effort in this area can produce great dividends. In today's computer age, e-mail can be a great tool of communication between father and son.

"A counselor suggested that I write a letter to my son Derek," recalled one father. "It was very hard for me. But with a little prompting from my wife, I sat down and wrote out my honest thoughts about how I was feeling. I told Derek about my own background. When I was a child, my dad's direct involvement with me was nil. But it didn't bother me. I knew he loved me, but he did shift work and labored long hours. I've also had to work shifts with lots of overtime, so I wasn't there for my son. But working was my way of showing him love. It had worked for me, and it seemed fine with my other kids. But it was a problem for Derek, and I had to accept that fact. I still feel guilty about it."

A few months later, Derek went home for a visit. He and his father sat down for a long talk. "There were a lot of tears and hugging," this father says. "I told him, 'You are my son and I love you, no matter what.' My son said he forgave me for any mistakes in the past, and I could tell he really meant it. I was walking on cloud nine when we were finished. But I still struggle with forgiving myself."

Commonly, fathers struggle to demonstrate unconditional love to their sons. They withhold approval until their son's behavior is "worthy" of being rewarded. This behavior can lead to a deep-seated rejection complex in the son. "I could never do enough for my father" is a common complaint among gay men. "If I brought home a B on my report card, he wanted to know why it wasn't an A. I never felt that he was very happy with anything I did."

Different interests can drive father and son apart. Typically, a father is crazy about sports and wants his son to share his same interests. When his son prefers music lessons and art classes, the father wonders how to relate. This sense of alienation is compounded tenfold when another brother *is* sports-minded and succeeds on the playing field. A step toward healing your relationship with an adult son is to seek out shared activities that both of you can enjoy.

One son who wished to get closer to his father knew that his dad had always enjoyed baseball. The son lived in a major city, near the home stadium of one of the top teams that season. So when his parents came to visit, this man suggested that he and his father attend a game. The father was eager to go.

Later the son explained how much the day had meant to him. "Finally Dad and I were doing something together—just the two of us. It was great. I'll never love baseball as much as he does, but being with him more than made up for any lack of interest on my part." Simple activities shared together can build important emotional bridges to help repair fractured family relationships.

A father may have a persistent disgust for the whole subject of homosexuality, even when it occurs in his own son. He may fear the negative reactions of his male buddies when his son's homosexuality becomes known. Unfortunately, all Christians have been influenced by secular culture. And homosexuality elicits strong abhorrence among many men today, despite growing support for gay rights in the popular media. These attitudes take a long time to unlearn. Ask God to make you willing to learn a new level of love for your son. Start by thanking God for your son and the qualities in him that you know are positive. You may be surprised how this opens the door for a deeper love and relationship.

Verbal approval is also important. "I love you" are three of the hardest words for a man to tell another man. "Of course I love him," one father sputtered. "He knows that—I don't have to tell him!" Unfortunately he's wrong. His son needs to hear those words, and to hear them often. Another father, only half-joking, says, "I told him that I loved him when he was born. If he doesn't remember, that's his problem." Leaders of ex-gay ministries often say that this is one of the most common statements from their male clients: "I don't remember my father ever telling me that he loved me."

When fathers begin reaching out with renewed effort, they may be disappointed to sense rejection from their sons. This wall may seem impossible to penetrate. Sons seem to be saying, "I don't care what you think. You weren't there when I needed you. So who needs you now?" Fathers need to understand the underlying message: "I will reject you so that you can't hurt me again." It's a protective device that will take consistent effort to eradicate. We can be at peace when we are doing our part to heal this important relationship in our son's life.

Mothers and Daughters

"I never felt like I met with Mom's approval," Pam said, tears streaming down her cheeks. During a counseling session, Pam was getting in touch with some painful memories from childhood. "No matter what I did, it never seemed quite enough. There was a lot of competition between us—we were both actively competing for my father's love. It always felt like I was trying to be as good as her. And I could never make it."

Pam was a mature woman who had left the lesbian life many years ago. She had a great marriage and enjoyed her role as wife and mother, but this area of her past was still painful for her.

The lesbian daughter often senses something missing in her relationship with her mother. The little girl grows up without a true sense of nurturing. For a multitude of reasons, she and her mother don't make a strong emotional connection. So the daughter begins an unconscious search for a woman to nurture her.

Eleanor always felt a sense of separation from her mother: "I don't remember any particular event which fostered this emotional distance. It was more of an inability to communicate honestly with each other that furthered the sense of separation I was experiencing.

"As I grew up, I remember spending much of my time observing my mother rather than connecting with her emotionally. I knew that I was meant to feel something about this woman who washed and ironed my clothes, fed me and gave me spending money. But I did not. Sometimes I would try to muster up a feeling. But I could not. Emotionally, I was numb."[3]

In other cases, the daughter goes through a traumatic experience (such as abuse or rape) and feels like her mother has abandoned her emotionally during the crisis. Afterward, the daughter finds it difficult to reconnect emotionally with her mother.

Sometimes the root of the daughter-mother breakdown is completely unintentional, perhaps something unavoidable. One woman remembers her mother's trip to a nearby town when her younger brother went into the hospital for emergency surgery. "I slept with her robe because it smelled like her. I couldn't understand why she had left me. I felt completely abandoned." As an adult, this woman understood that it was appropriate for her mother to stay with her little brother during that time. She recognized the reasons behind her mother's action, but she still felt the emotional abandonment and didn't know how to erase that inner pain.

Many lesbians see their mothers as weak, ineffective and unaffirming of the daughter's femininity. The mother may also be perceived as manipulative, lying to her husband to get what she wants without standing up to him. The mother's passive "peace-at-all-costs" type of behavior can give the daughter wrong ideas about a wife's proper role in the home. The young girl thinks, *If that's what being a woman is all about, I don't want any part of it.*

This was Mickey's experience. She was a lesbian woman with a rough exterior. Her mother, Vera, had been badly abused by an alcoholic husband. When Mickey was young, she would help her mother up off the floor after Vera had been shoved around by her husband. Mickey remembers vowing, "I'll get even with him someday." In her teens, she would defend her mother physically as much as possible when her dad came home drunk.

After Mickey left home, she tried to talk her mother into leaving with her, but Vera refused. She loved her husband despite the ongoing abuse. Mickey became very independent and competitive with both men and women. She felt secure only when she was in control of a situation or relationship. Mickey was denied comfort and protection from her mother because of the tumult occurring in their home. Mickey developed a love-hate relationship with her mom, always wishing Vera would stand up for herself and fight off her husband's abusive behavior. Only after

Mickey's father died of alcohol-related cirrhosis did she develop a closer, nonjudgmental relationship with her mother.

Other women dealing with lesbianism appeared to have a "perfect" relationship with their father. It was certainly stronger than the mother-daughter relationship. The child, as she grows, may identify strongly with her father, even to the extent of defending negative behavior on his part: "No wonder Daddy drank so much. Look at what he had to endure with Mother all those years!" This is an impossible situation for the "erring" parent. In this example, the mother can do no right, the father no wrong. Even if the father leaves the marriage, the daughter will say, "It's not his fault. Mother drove him away."

Many mothers are genuinely puzzled why their daughters turned to lesbianism. Their relationship seemed normal, even close. These mothers should pray that God will give them insight into this issue and an opportunity to discuss this subject with their daughter. It's difficult for parents to face the possibility that their past shortcomings may have impaired a daughter's development in some way.

A mother should look for the elements which may have been lacking in her relationship with her daughter and seek to discover new ways of connecting. It's difficult but helpful for the mother to initiate a discussion of the whole matter with her daughter. If a mother can listen to her daughter and show concern without being defensive or excusing herself, she will be doing her part to break through any emotional barriers that may exist.

If a mother has always been critical of her daughter, for example, she can strive to change that pattern by actively seeking ways to show affirmation. This can be a difficult challenge if the daughter is still involved in an immoral lifestyle. Pray that the Lord will show you specific traits in your daughter's life that you can compliment.

Keep in mind the distinction between *acceptance* (affirming the daughter as a person) and *approval* (affirming the daughter's behavior). Offering acceptance without approval will provide a healing atmosphere for your daughter's life. It's also helpful to keep reminding yourself to distinguish between what you are responsible for—your own attitudes and actions toward your daughter—and what you cannot control—your daughter's reactions toward you. If your daughter is angry and rebellious, those issues must be worked out between her and God. Your part is to love her and pray for God to continue working in her life.

Fathers and Daughters

It's not unusual for lesbian daughters to have had a close relationship with their father. Sometimes they bond with Dad, almost to the exclusion of a relationship with the mother.

"I was always Daddy's little helper," one woman admitted. "I used to tag along behind him, no matter what he was doing. He'd let me hold the wrench when he was fixing the car. I would sit next to him for hours, quietly amusing myself with his tools while he tinkered away on his project."

Another woman described how she had grown up as her father's "buddy." They talked about everything together, even to the extent that her dad began confiding in her about his marital problems. "The things he shared were pretty personal," she recalls. "But I didn't think twice about taking his side. Soon it became our private little joke." As an adult, this woman realized that this dynamic with her father hindered her from bonding with her mother. She had to accept her mother just the way she was, owning up to her part in the father-daughter relationship which had helped her to detach emotionally from her mother.

A young girl's relationship with her dad is usually motivated by a search for his approval. If affirmation as "Daddy's little girl" is lacking, she may attempt to find favor by being *like* her father. She will begin adopting his interests and sharing his hobbies, dropping her natural identification with the feminine. Sometimes this rejection of the female is reinforced by one or both parents.

At the other extreme is the daughter who felt rejected by her father. "My parents made no secret of the fact that they wanted a boy," said Roberta, the youngest of four girls. "They picked out the name Robert, then reluctantly added the *a* on the end when I was born." During her years of involvement in lesbian relationships, Roberta rejected anything associated with the feminine. Her favorite outfit was a man's flannel shirt, jeans and army boots. This woman was playing out her parents' expectations, even though it meant rejecting her true identity as a woman.

Daughters also pick up many clues about their feminine role through observing their father's attitude toward their mother. If the relationship is negative or abusive, this sets up a conflict within the developing child. She will associate being feminine with being hurt and may begin to reject typical feminine clothing and activities.

Some fathers have unintentionally distanced themselves from daughters by projecting a macho-type image that alienates their daughter. One burly father used to bellow, "If anyone ever hurts my little girl, I'll kill him!" His young daughter saw how big he was and took his words literally. When, as a young teen, she was molested by an older male, she kept silent. "I was terrified that Dad would kill the man who abused me," she said, "and then I would be responsible for murder. So I kept silent—for years." She was an adult and had come out of her lesbian lifestyle before she had the courage to confess her past to her father.[4]

We rarely get inquiries from fathers with lesbian daughters, so we've had little chance to see common patterns within this relationship. Other parent-child dynamics (for example, the way a mother relates to her gay son) are far more predictable. In our experience, a daughter's lesbian pursuits are more commonly triggered by traumatic events—usually physical, emotional or sexual abuse—than by any other single factor.

Unbalanced Relationships in the Family

Few homes have perfectly balanced relationships. Often a gay child is closest to the opposite-sex parent and more distant from the same-sex parent. Sometimes it is helpful to look at this situation from the child's perspective. As a parent, I have learned a lot from the people I have counseled over the years.

I remember Lisa, who had been overcoming her lesbian past for about two years. "I've recently realized that my mom wasn't the whole problem," she told me one day, "even though she was a little crazy and not very dependable when I was growing up." Lisa sat across from me, looking down at the floor.

I tried to affirm the important steps toward healing that she had already made in her life. "Yes, Lisa. But you have learned a lot about accepting her just the way she is now."

She nodded slightly. "But Dad was the one I could depend on. He was my rock. Now I realize that he has a lot of problems too. The way he always confided in me about Mom's problems wasn't right."

Lisa continued to process these issues during the coming months. Through getting in touch with many conflicting emotions about her parents, she came to a better understanding of her mother's problems when Lisa was a child. It hurt to realize that her father had contributed to the problem by confiding improperly in her, instead of seeking counsel from an appropriate adult. Now Lisa had to give up some of the idealistic image she'd always had of her father. Instead, she was making efforts to become better acquainted with her heavenly Father, who would never let her down. With God's help, she was also working to repair her relationship with her mother.

In fact, her relationship with both parents was becoming more realistic. As she became more dependent on God for her emotional security, she felt less angry at her parents. Each day it became a little easier to accept both of them, even while acknowledging their faults. She saw how they had given her their best at the time. Lisa began looking for ways to affirm their strengths without criticizing their weaknesses.

Marital Pressures

When parents learn about their gay child, usually one of them takes the leading role in attempting to "rescue" the child. This may leave the other parent feeling frustrated and jealous. A husband may be upset because he realizes that such rescuing behavior is not in the child's best interest. He may be jealous because the mother is so focused on the needs of the child, and puzzled because he would like to take a more active role in helping the child, but doesn't know how.

Or the nonrescuing parent will become even more firm in an attempt to counterbalance the permissive parent. Typically, with a gay son, the father withdraws from the situation, leaving the mother to intervene. This is disastrous for the son, who desperately needs love from his father. And the different reactions on the parents' part can confuse the son. The whole situation can drive parents apart, just at a time when they need strong support from each other.

Parents must be careful to guard their marriage. This situation brings tremendous stress into their relationship. If they do not approach it with a united front, a child's homosexuality can destroy the foundation of their marriage. Sometimes parents will seek professional counseling in order to adequately process this time of grief, frustration and pain.

Facing the Crisis Alone

Living with the knowledge that your child is a homosexual is difficult even when you can rely on your spouse's support. But going it alone is a greater challenge. You may be a single parent. Or you may be married to an unsaved spouse. You might even be married to a Christian husband or wife who believes that homosexuality is "no big deal" and does not support your position against this behavior.

Single parents and those who are married to unbelieving spouses often feel guilty for not providing the "perfect" marriage and family situation for their child. Even though the dynamics of the situation could have been set in place years before their commitment to Christ, these parents continue to feel remorse. I raised Tony as a single mother, and I still remember scolding myself, "If I had married when I had the chance . . ." But thousands of gay men and women come from two-parent homes; an intact marriage is no guarantee that children will be perfect!

Certainly there is added pressure when you don't have the support of a Christian spouse. It can be even more difficult to have an outspoken spouse who has a radically different opinion on the morality of homosexual behavior. How can you maintain your biblical standards when your partner is too liberal in thinking? Parents in these circumstances need to make an extra effort to get steady encouragement from outside the home. Some pair up with other parents through letters or phone calls to ease the burden of a gay child. Others live close enough to attend a specialized support group.

Loneliness is common. It's easy to become isolated. Single parents often work a full-time job, then have the responsibilities of shopping, household chores, church involvement—*and* spending quality time with their kids! Who has time for a social life? Those with unsaved spouses can also feel isolated because the unbeliever is not comfortable with their Christian friends. It's tempting to escape into a fantasy world of soap operas, romance novels or just daydreaming. But when we return to the real world, it seems even more miserable than before.

Loneliness and self-pity feed into each other. When Tony was small, I went through a difficult period. I felt an urgent need to talk to an adult, and found myself phoning my married brother—my one and only support person. Eventually I realized that I was taking him away from important family time, and I stopped my frequent calls. But then I would sit by the phone and cry; I felt so alone and sad because I didn't have a family. Who could share my growing concerns about my son?

Now I realize that someone in my situation should form a strong spiritual support team. I was too busy for consistent times alone with the Lord. But I desperately needed God. I needed to be asking him for advice and seeking the answers in his Word. And I needed to spend time building quality friendships, rather than depending on just one person. I was in ministry to single mothers back then, but I lacked friends who were my equals. I needed to be more open with the leaders in my church. This would have prevented a lot of my loneliness, misery and self-pity.

Parenting: The Ongoing Challenge

The challenges of being a parent are ongoing, and many other parents face similar battles to yours. Remember that the Lord willingly "daily bears our burdens" (Psalm 68:19). In Isaiah 41 he reminds us, "I am the LORD, your God, who takes hold of your right hand and says to you, Do not fear; I will help you" (v. 13).

Parenting is never easy. But as one mother says, "Despite any mistakes I have made in the past, God has been faithful. I can confidently face the future, knowing that my family is living under his watchful care."[5] May the Lord grant you this same assurance.

9
Just for Spouses: Special Concerns & Questions

S heila Hood had detected symptoms of a deep conflict in her husband's life since the beginning of their marriage. In public, Bill was usually calm and gentle. In the privacy of their home, he was often moody, withdrawn and violently angry.

There were other signs of a hidden problem: the times he would slip his wedding ring back on his finger after returning from an especially late night in the city . . . the way his eyes met with those of total strangers . . . the preoccupation he had with his outward appearance that had nothing to do with pleasing his wife. Sheila sensed a growing distance between them. Finally, after two years of marriage, she had to know the truth.

"Bill, there's something I must ask you." She paused to take a deep breath, as if it would give her an added measure of courage. "What keeps you at a distance from me day after day and night after night? Is there something deeply wrong?"

At first Bill said nothing. He just stared, without expression. Finally he broke the incredible silence.

"There's something I haven't told you," he admitted. "I have this terrible battle raging inside of me all the time. It's not against you. It's just that I, well, it's just that I prefer to be with men."

"Do you mean intimately, sexually?" Sheila felt her heart crushing inside her.

"Yes." Bill lowered his gaze toward the floor. "But recently, it's just been the thoughts."

As the implication of his words sank in, Sheila started trembling. "You mean you've been involved sexually with men since we were married?" The tears were hot on her face as Bill admitted the truth.

In the days to come, Sheila stood by her husband, believing that God could heal anything. Bill seemed almost as perplexed as she did about his struggles. Neither of them felt equipped to deal with his inner turmoil. But Sheila was confident that fervent prayer would put this problem behind them.[1]

Double Life

Suddenly you find out that your spouse has been living a double life. Your home, so stable the day before, now seems like it is collapsing around you. This discovery ripples through your home like a California earthquake, leaving emotional devastation everywhere. How can you go on?

It's important for spouses to remember that, almost always, *homosexuality predates a marriage*. Its roots are usually sown in childhood, even though it bears fruit in adulthood. Some spouses have struggled with homosexual issues in the past, then hoped that they were delivered forever. But if the root issues underlying the homosexual condition were never totally severed, the symptoms can resurface at a later date, even after marriage.

Homosexual struggles in a husband's life point to an *ongoing same-sex deficit*. This deficit often manifests itself as a craving for sex with another man. The pull seems irresistible, like an alcoholic yearning for a drink.

This problem is not the fault of his wife. It has little—if anything—to do with her appearance, behavior or personality. In the overwhelming majority of cases, she is an innocent bystander in an unfolding tragedy. Often the trigger to a husband's actual fall into sexual sin is a factor outside the marriage, such as work-related stress. For a Christian, it can also be spiritually based.

One former minister remembers why his first marriage broke up in the mid-1970s: "My life as a pastor centered around the ministry. Although I loved Heather and we had a normal sex life, our marriage was empty. All we ever did was minister, minister, minister."

After four years this pastor got disillusioned with his church position and resigned. He started working a secular job and became very disappointed when God didn't immediately open up another ministry position.

"As my bitterness increased, all the old homosexual feelings began to return," he admits. "I started falling in love with guys at work; one night, on a whim, I went into an adult bookstore. Soon I was right back into the old lifestyle." Within three months, his marriage had fallen apart. The root issue was his struggle with God—not a failure on the part of his wife.

For a wife, lesbian struggles are similarly rooted in *a deep need for same-sex affirmation.* A man can never fulfill this type of relational need. Often the wife is looking for another woman with whom she can connect emotionally at a deep level. In fact, married women may become emotionally entangled in a lesbian affair long before sexual involvement occurs. A common scenario is a healthy friendship that becomes a "best friend" situation, which leads to an overly close dependency that becomes sexualized.[2]

The situation can come upon the unsuspecting husband so fast that he is totally unaware of any problem. Here's how one young husband described it: "I thought we were happy. Then, out of nowhere, she announced that she was going off with her friend. 'Pam understands me, but you never have' is how she summarized the whole situation."

This dynamic is recognized by counselors who offer support to married women with a lesbian background. "Many married women complain that their husband can't meet their emotional needs," says Carol Fryer, a counselor in Toronto, Ontario. "There is a lot of non-verbal communication between two close women friends. She knows my needs, I don't have to say them to her. I don't even have to understand them myself. She can tell me how I feel. My husband can't do that for me because he doesn't have that same intuition."[3] This powerful empathy can draw two needy women into inappropriate physical involvement.

Issues for Wives

The woman whose husband is involved in a homosexual struggle is usually consumed with fear. She has a gut-level instinct that he is being unfaithful, but she is not sure. She goes to bed alone, then lies awake for hours, waiting, praying, crying. "I don't trust my husband," said a woman after her husband confessed to one incident of adultery. "Every time he's late, I think, *Here we go again.*"

Many wives feel totally alone. Family and friends don't know about these agonizing nights. Whom could she tell? Those close to her would hate her husband for the misery he is putting her through. She wonders if it is better to keep quiet and protect the marriage. Maybe things will improve soon and her husband will be grateful that nobody else found out.

Sometimes the wife decides to tell someone else, such as her mother or a close girlfriend. She may get poor advice, such as "You should leave him immediately!" or "You are crazy for staying." In today's society many people have lost sight of God's standard for a lifelong commitment in marriage. A wife who has a strong desire to stay and work it out can be baffled by all the contrary advice she receives from friends and spiritual leaders.

But often a wife is not motivated primarily by spiritual reasons for staying in her marriage. Fear may be her main motivation to stay. This fear can take many forms.

Fear of losing income. If there are children and the wife is not working outside the home, the family is dependent on the husband's income to survive. If the wife has little training for outside employment, she can feel overwhelmed at the thought of supporting her family on a low income.

Fear of being alone. For married women, the thought of being single is scary, especially the prospect of raising children alone. The dread of future loneliness can be overwhelming. *Will I ever be loved again?* a wife may wonder.

Fear of humiliation. There is certainly a shame factor in being married to a homosexual. It's embarrassing to think of this secret being brought out into the open.

Issues for Husbands

Stan Harris was a newlywed when he sensed that something was different about his wife's same-sex relationships. She seemed to spend a lot of time investing in her female friendships, and they seemed so all-consuming. And there was a lot of affection demonstrated that seemed excessive to Stan. He started to panic. *What am I doing wrong?* he wondered. *Is she a lesbian? No, it can't be true.* He couldn't accept what his mind was telling him. He felt scared—and trapped.

They eventually began talking about the subject. "My wife tried to explain how she related to women, and why the relationships got so intense," Stan remembers. "While I was listening, I didn't have a clue what she was talking about. But I sensed that the issue she was discussing wasn't just going to disappear on its own." Over the next few years, he saw his wife struggling with emotionally dependent relationships with several women. She was bonding emotionally with same-sex friends in a way that made Stan very uncomfortable.

God seemed far away in the midst of Stan's turmoil. "I felt alone. I had no answers. I didn't even know where to turn."[4]

Some men, during a time of emotional stress, are tempted to escape into an affair. Another man described how when his wife spent time in counseling to seek healing from her lesbian past, he would feel a "magnetic attraction toward other women." Usually he and his wife experienced events together, he explained, with their shared feelings of joy or sorrow, excitement or pleasure. But this was an area of his wife's life that he could not share, even though he was supportive of her therapy. So his feelings of emotional separation from her turned into a strong attraction for other women. "There was a definite pattern that I came to recognize," he said.

The husband tends to focus more on his own sexual fulfillment than looking at what his wife's behavior is really indicating. "I had to learn how to meet my wife's emotional needs," Stan admits. "This area of emotional need is so foreign to most men. But meeting her on that level was the 'glue' in our marriage, according to her perspective." In ignorance, a husband may mistakenly try to win his wife back through sexual seduction, rather than through emotional attachment.

Healthy Reasons to Stay

We mentioned several negative fears that motivate a wife to remain in the marriage. Of course, there are also positive reasons why both husbands and wives stay married.

Children's well-being. If there are children in the family, a husband or wife may choose to stay for their sake. Studies have repeatedly shown the devastation brought into children's lives when their parents divorce.[5]

Spiritual influence. By remaining in the marriage, a husband or wife will be closer to the spouse and can more easily detect their needs and struggles. A husband or wife can pray in more specific and timely ways for the struggling spouse. Also, the Christian partner can show Christ's unconditional love day by day, with the hope that a godly influence will help persuade the spouse to turn his or her life around and be obedient to God's laws of sexual purity.

Divine revelation. The most important reason to remain in a marriage is this one: God's Word strongly promotes lifelong commitment. Perhaps during times of prayer, the "straight" husband or wife has sensed an unshakable hope for the future of their marriage. Only the Lord can see the hidden motives of the soul. He can see the future and what it holds. And his heart is always directed toward unity and reconciliation.

Stay Together or Separate?

If a marriage is becoming intolerable, the first step to consider is temporary separation. This action is a very serious step to contemplate. Sometimes physical abuse or other intolerable circumstances are occurring which make the choice rather obvious. In other homes, the factors are subtle, and the options are confusing.

Here are some symptoms which *may* indicate that separation is an option to consider:

☐ The gay spouse is spending major unaccounted time away from the family.

☐ The gay spouse appears to have given up trying to solve the homosexual problem. One lesbian wife flaunted her "special friendship" with another woman to her husband and refused to heed his pleas to separate.

☐ The gay spouse (especially in the case of a husband) shows a constant disregard for his partner's physical and sexual health. Both men and women can bring incurable diseases into the marriage from another sexual partner. For example, the husband can infect his wife with HIV, which is fatal.

☐ The gay spouse blames his or her partner for all the problems occurring in the marriage and refuses rational discussion.

☐ The gay spouse is engaging in other destructive behavior, such as heavy drinking or illegal drug usage.

☐ The gay spouse exhibits a pattern of habitual deception. "I hated the lying more than his running around," said one wife. "I began to doubt my discernment. I would confront my husband and he'd retort, 'How could you think such a thing about me?' " Later this wife discovered that her suspicions were correct. Her husband was not ready to change his ways.

A wife struggling with lesbianism may never commit sexual adultery with another woman, but she can get into destructive emotional relationships ("crushes") with other women. These death-grip relationships are just as addictive to the wife as a gay husband's physical adultery with other men.

Separation should *not* be viewed as a sign that one or both spouses have given up on the marriage. Ultimately, it can be one step toward reconciliation, especially when the gay spouse is leaving the family to seek specialized help.

Jenny and Kevin had reached an impasse in their marriage. Kevin's homosexual behavior seemed to get more out of control each day. Jenny had no hope for their future together. They agreed it was best for Kevin to leave the area and get help elsewhere. Meanwhile, they would both pray that God would put their marriage back together.

Jenny and Kevin were separated for the next year. She lived in Illinois; Kevin spent the twelve months in a residential treatment center for Christians struggling with homosexuality. During that year, Kevin explored the underlying issues which had led him into homosexuality in the first place. He also had strict accountability and maintained freedom from homosexual acts for the entire year. Back in Illinois, Jenny was finding out more about herself too, such as the reasons she had been attracted to Kevin's passivity and how she contributed to his problems with her dominating personality.

Kevin eventually moved back to his home city. He lived for three months in an apartment while he and his wife "dated," spending time together discussing what they had learned during their year apart. Today, over eight years later, this couple is happily married with two children. Their period of physical separation did not spell the end of their marriage. They had good reasons to separate, and they had solid spiritual input while they were apart. God laid a new foundation for their relationship, and now they have a good marriage.

From this illustration, we see that a time of separation can benefit a troubled marriage. Such a separation can signal the beginning of a new chapter in the couple's lives. There are potential pitfalls, but there can also be great gains. It can work only if, like Kevin and Jenny, both spouses are committed to working on issues in their respective lives which may be contributing to the difficulties in their relationship.

Separation can also open the door to one spouse's receiving specialized help in another geographical area, such as specific counseling for men or women overcoming homosexuality.

Separation can also provide a time for the gay spouse to evaluate life apart from the other spouse's influence. Freedom from the usual responsibilities of marriage and family can provide a new perspective. A husband may be surprised to discover that his triggers to temptation are still firmly in place, even without his wife around (previously he blamed her behavior for causing his struggles). A wife may discover just how much she misses her children and husband, even though she never realized it before. Loneliness, grief, feelings of abandonment, separation anxiety, identity crises—all of these possible emotional reactions can ultimately be beneficial in giving a new appreciation for one's marriage. A husband who lived a double life now knows what his life would be like without his wife and children. Before, he was slipping out to fulfill his fantasies, then sneaking home to the comforts and company of his family. Some men confront, for the first time, the possibility of losing their wife and children. The impact of that discovery gives a renewed determination to make the marriage work.

Although we see success stories, we don't want to be unrealistic in discussing this subject. Jim Talley, author of *Reconcilable Differences* and a marital and family therapist who has counseled hundreds of troubled couples, says that about 30 percent of separated couples eventually go on to get divorced.[6] Without a high degree of motivation and unconditional surrender to God's will by both partners, the prospect of a renewed marriage is low.

Even a husband's successful exit from homosexuality does not guarantee that a marriage will prosper. Ron and Elaine's marriage had been limping along for over fifteen years. Ron had fallen into several homosexual relationships during that time; he had been free of adultery for over five years but still struggled with strong same-sex attractions. For the past few years he and his wife had lived in the same house but occupied separate bedrooms. They were in a stable financial situation, and the children were grown. Then Ron heard about a residential program on the East Coast for men overcoming homosexuality, and they agreed that he should relocate there to enter the program.

During the next year, Ron thrived in the program and enjoyed his time with other men dealing with similar problems. Toward the end of the program, Elaine flew out to visit and receive some counseling herself. The program leader tried to help them see the value of their marriage and what steps they could take to heal their relationship. But everyone noticed that Ron acted very uncomfortable around his wife; several days later, she went home feeling rejected and disappointed.

During the next few months, it was apparent that Ron enjoyed his single life and had no desire to reconcile with his wife. He seemed relieved to escape the pressures of his marriage and the gossip of the small town where he and Elaine had lived. He would not even consider reconciliation unless his wife would move to a new area, but she did not want to leave her friends and family. Neither partner was willing to compromise on the matter, and they continued to live apart. Now, five years later, they are divorced.

Ron's situation is ironic. He left homosexuality successfully—but still had no desire to work on his marriage. There are many reasons why separated couples do not reconcile, and the painful process of facing an uncertain future can be excruciating. If you are in this situation, we recommend the excellent book *Separated and Waiting* by Jan Northington (Thomas Nelson, 1994) as a practical and encouraging resource.

Finding Hope

We have spelled out some behaviors which may be cause for concern, even physical separation. Now let's look at the opposite situation, where there are signs that a troubled marriage is moving in the right direction.

☐ The gay spouse begins avoiding unnecessary homosexual temptation. A struggling husband will avoid stores that sell gay pornography, as well as areas of town where homosexuals "cruise" for sexual partners. A struggling wife will seek balance in her relationships rather than always spending time with only one "best" friend. She will include several women in her close circle of friends.

☐ The gay spouse takes some concrete steps toward personal spiritual growth. Without nagging from others, a husband will seek insight from the Lord during times spent alone in Bible reading and prayer. He might offer to pray with his wife for their mutual struggles, or begin attending church with his family.

☐ The gay spouse desires accountability. This step could involve finding one or two persons to meet with regularly for mutual encouragement. Some will join an ex-gay support group in their city. Others will begin counseling with a pastor or Christian professional.

☐ The gay spouse exhibits a willingness to work at improving the marriage. There will be a desire to talk about the difficulties and changes that both partners need to make. Other couples will attend a "marriage encounter" weekend or seek specialized help for troubled marriages.

Nongay spouses often seek spiritual counsel, then get confused when they get conflicting advice. One person may say, "You must leave if your husband has committed adultery. He could give you AIDS!" Another counselor may sternly advise the wife, "No matter what happens, stay in your marriage. God will honor your submissive obedience."

Perhaps you are puzzled about whom you can seek for the proper support. Here are some suggestions on how to get the best advice.

Look for input from people who are supportive of your marriage. The Bible is blunt: God hates divorce (Malachi 2:16). Those who give quick advice to break up a marriage are not encouraging you to consider God's perspective on this subject. Nor are they being sensitive to the deep commitment which you may have toward your marriage. Although divorce is a reality in modern churches of every denomination, it is not the first option to pursue even for a marriage threatened by homosexuality.

Look for input from people who have known both you and your spouse over a long time period. Someone who has never met your spouse before can get a perspective from you which may not be the most balanced in the long run. Firsthand observation of a person's actions over a period of time is a far better indicator of character and a better predictor of future actions.

Look for input from people who understand the root causes and healing of homosexuality. Many people do not believe that homosexuality or lesbianism can be resolved. But thousands of men and women have successfully overcome this situation, and many of them are happily married.[7] A homosexual problem does not necessitate divorce. Many spouses who have wrestled with this issue have maintained their marriage; some even minister now to others caught in the same predicament.

When a Spouse Leaves

In 1981, a little ministry was born that brought hope to hundreds of women whose husbands had left them for male lovers. The Door of Hope was founded by two wives whose husbands had left, but these women were "standing for" their marriages. They believed, no matter what the circumstances, that their husbands would eventually return and their marriages would be restored. Divorce was never an option for them as Christians—period.

"If you believe that you married the man God had for you, you can know that his perfect will is to restore your marriage and deliver your husband," one wife wrote in their newsletter. The two women leading Door of Hope found Scriptures like Luke 1:37 ("Nothing is impossible with God") to hang on to, claiming that God had already redeemed their marriages.

As the years passed, however, both women were forced to reexamine their beliefs. They were loosely linked with the national ministry of "Born-Again Marriages," whose participants were standing for their marriages even when their spouse had been gone for years and had married someone else. Both of these women married to actively gay men began wondering what they really believed.

The two women eventually realized that due to the long absence of their husbands and the fact that neither man had made any move in the direction of renouncing his homosexuality, God was releasing them from their commitment to wait for the return of their husbands. They believed that some wives could continue to intercede for their mate's return, but others were free to seek divorce and move on with their lives.

Some critics said the women didn't have enough faith or did not take enough time reading their "affirmation cards" filled with Bible verses that promised restoration. But these women disagreed. "Whatever the problem, it wasn't that I had a lack of faith," one argued. "I just think there's a time to let somebody go."

Her friend added, "If your husband has turned away completely, then you have to accept that reality. He's made his choice."

Here's how the women summarized their current beliefs: "Wives are really wanting the 'good old days' to come back, the days before they knew about the problem. In actuality, there probably weren't any 'good old days' because the marriage was filled with lying and cover-up, silence and lack of communication on a variety of issues. That marriage shouldn't be restored. It needs a complete rebuilding from the ground up."[8]

The issues of separation and divorce remain highly emotional topics in evangelical churches today. However, an increasing number of Christians *are* divorced, which has dramatically affected the way churches deal with this situation. To stay in balance, we can remember that although God hates divorce, Jesus allowed for it in cases of sexual unfaithfulness (Matthew 19:9).

One couple who have spent many years counseling other couples encourage a spouse to always make a solid attempt to restore the relationship before abandoning it. "A common thread of anxiety runs through people who are divorced and then remarried," say Jim and Sally Conway in their book *Moving On After He Moves Out.* "Three or four years into the next marriage, when everything is not as wonderful as was hoped, the partners begin to ask themselves, *Could I have saved my first marriage if I had worked harder?* and *How much did I contribute to the breakup of my marriage?*"[9] But when substantial efforts have been made to restore the first marriage and it still does not come back together, the Conways say, these people have a genuine sense of freedom as they move on into other relationships.

"It took me a couple of years after my husband left before I filed for divorce," said one woman whose spouse moved in with another man. "I needed to figure out who I was apart from my husband. I felt so utterly powerless. Pursuing divorce was an active step that I could take to re-gain control of my life. I knew I'd given him lots of time, and the situation was not going to change."

Sheila Hood, whose story began this chapter, eventually reached the same decision to divorce her husband, Bill, after an extended consultation with her pastor. "It wasn't an easy step to take," she said. "In 13 years of pleading, praying, and despairing, I had always been very sure divorce was not an option. I had made a vow. I meant to keep it. Unfortunately, Bill never did. My pastor heard me through, then confirmed my right under God to divorce and to remarry."[10] She and Bill separated, although they remained in periodic contact. About ten years after their divorce, Bill died of AIDS-related illness. Sheila has remained single and a contented mother to her one daughter.

We believe that the issue of when and if to pursue divorce is a life-changing decision that should be considered only after thorough discussion with others who can give you godly direction. We encourage you to receive input from your pastor or other spiritual mentors who can give realistic yet biblical counsel. Whatever decision is made, you will need lots of emotional support as you move ahead with your life.

When Your Husband Struggles

We have already tried to make it clear: Your husband's problem is *his* problem, not yours. And his problem with homosexuality probably pre-dated your marriage. You didn't cause it, and you can't fix it.

But there is an area where you can be responsible: your own actions and attitudes. All of us have areas of our lives which are wounded and need God's healing.

Usually when one spouse has a grievous sin struggle, all the attention focuses on helping him or her solve *the* problem. In some ways, this makes it easier on you. You're just the "innocent" party in all this (or so it would be nice to believe). But even though you haven't been responsible for your spouse's homosexual struggles, you can still seek your own growth during this time in order to become a better marital partner for the future.

Growth is painful for us all. But there are also wonderful blessings when our hearts are tender. We need the healing touch of Jesus in our lives. He loves us and desires us to be all that we can be through his power.

Growth occurs when we take an honest look at our past. Often the wife of a homosexual man has a whole set of areas that need healing. There may have been hurts in your life that drew you to your husband, especially if you knew of his homosexuality and married him anyway.

Here are some common characteristics which might need healing.

Low self-esteem. Often the woman who is drawn to a man with problems believes that she doesn't deserve a whole and healthy husband. She feels that no man would love her unless he needed her. She doesn't consciously look for a man with problems. But she consistently tends to be drawn to the same type of person, such as a drinker or an abuser. This clue would be especially relevant if you have fallen into this situation on more than one occasion, such as in a previous marriage or through several boyfriends who all "happened" to be gay. Such a pattern may reflect a woman's damaged self-respect: "This man won't expect much from me because his problems are so great."

Attraction to passive men. This type of woman may have suffered abuse from men during her youth. She feels threatened by men she cannot dominate and control. So she is drawn to males who are soft, gentle and passive.

Needing to fix problems. This woman is always drawn to a man who needs her help. She has a deep need to be needed. Her childhood home may have been chaotic. In an alcoholic home, for example, she held things together for her siblings and offered support to the nonalcoholic parent.

Some wives have come from an abusive home, and they drift toward abusive relationships as adults. Being abused is horrible, but it's familiar. She has dealt with it in the past, and she knows how to respond.

These examples may or may not apply to your life. But an honest examination of your past will help you ascertain what areas of your life need God's touch in order for you to become a healthy wife. If you and your husband have been in dysfunctional roles, you will be thrown off course as he moves into his rightful place. If he was consistently passive and now begins to express his opinion on disciplining the children, this will be a new challenge to face together.

Every wife wants her husband to stop having sex outside the marriage. But not every wife wants him to take his proper role in the marriage. A godly wife, however, will welcome the changes that come from true healing and will encourage her husband in the midst of the changes that come.

Janet was thrilled that her husband, Wayne, was finally getting the help he needed. She had prayed for so long, and now it was happening! But as the months went by and Wayne's behavior began to change, Janet grew increasingly fearful. Quite frankly, things seemed to be getting worse. She felt like she was losing him. They seemed to have more conflicts than ever. Wayne was confronting her on things that had never been a problem before—or so it seemed. He mentioned on several occasions that he felt "mothered" by her, which she found offensive. He'd always welcomed her direction in the past. What was going on?

Wayne gave quite a different perspective to his counselor: "When I'm with Janet, I feel like the same old person: a boy instead of a man. Janet wants me to 'need' her in the same way that I used to. But I don't. Things are changing. And I'm afraid that staying with her will drive me right back into homosexuality." Wayne *did* leave his wife eventually, although he didn't return to homosexual behavior. If Janet had been willing to seek healing in her own life at the same time that Wayne was changing, their marriage might have been saved.

It's vitally important for wives to get in touch with their anger and begin to process it. "In your anger do not sin," the Bible admonishes in Ephesians 4:26. Many churches teach that anger itself is sin. But that is not what the Bible says here. This passage says that anger exists, but we can deal with it in a godly fashion by controlling the ways that we express it. Releasing your anger in appropriate ways gets it out into the open where it can be processed.

Anger has been a big issue for Willa Medinger, whose husband was sexually unfaithful with other men before his conversion to Christ in 1974. Since 1979, Willa and her husband, Alan, have ministered to hundreds of other couples struggling with the issue of homosexuality within marriage. "Have the courage to *feel* your anger and pain," Willa advises wives in troubled marriages. "You have to walk through it, not around it. There is no other way to find release and freedom. You'll be chained for the rest of your life."

Willa's anger came out after her husband had broken away from homosexuality. Alan was dramatically healed of homosexual inclinations and has remained faithful to her for over twenty years. But Willa still had to process her anger over the past. Shortly after Alan's deliverance, Willa had returned home with him from church. During a subsequent discussion, Willa found herself beating Alan on the chest with her fists, screaming, "I hate you, I hate you, I hate you!" Finally, her emotions spent, she slumped down on the couch and fell into an exhausted slumber.

"Think about your anger," she says. "Journal it. Talk about it. A marriage cannot move on until the anger from the lying and deceit is dealt with. And don't forget about your anger with God. In most wives, it's in there somewhere." Many women have prayed for their marriage before it even began. And now this disaster! Where has God been all these years? He *could* have stopped the problems before they got so bad—he is supposed to be all-powerful! These deep feelings of rage are hard to face; they are so "theologically incorrect" that many Christians bury them deep inside without even realizing that they exist.

Sometimes the anger takes years to surface. When Alan came out of homosexuality, he began loving Willa in a whole new way. But, she admits, she had not forgiven him deep in her heart. "Six years after Alan's healing, life went out of control for me. It became very apparent to those around me that I needed help. When I sought counseling, I spent hours talking about what had happened to *me*. Eventually Alan joined me for joint counseling, and I began to be honest with him about my anger." Finally, the counselor pointed out to Willa that her problems didn't begin with her marriage. Alan had been just one person in a long line of people who had taken advantage of her.

"I realized that I was determined to hold on to unforgiveness," she says. "It was my *right*. It was hard to really face this issue. But once I said the word—and admitted my unforgiveness—I felt this great release inside. It was a new beginning for me."[11]

When Your Wife Struggles

We have talked with many wives during our years of counseling, but few husbands have contacted us for help. Usually the marriage is in the last stages of dying before a man will call for assistance. Typically, a husband had never suspected his wife's vulnerability to this problem. The issue strikes like lightning from a clear sky. The husband is shocked, stunned, disbelieving. He often has no idea of how to proceed with the situation.

Here are a few other common symptoms among the husbands who have discovered their wife is involved with another woman.

Damaged male ego. A man tends to take his wife's lesbianism in a deeply personal way. It is offensive, shameful, a blow to his male ego that he—a "full-blooded male"—is not man enough to satisfy his wife's sexual desires.

Husbands are sensitive about what others will think, especially how they will be perceived by male friends. They worry that other men will question their masculinity if their wife is looking elsewhere for sexual fulfillment. A lot of their focus is on their own sexual abilities, needs and desirability. Their masculine ego is deeply wounded that their wife has rejected them sexually. They feel insecure about whether or not they are still physically attractive to their wife. In some cases, the real problem is that she was emotionally starving in the relationship, and she was susceptible when a sympathetic and affectionate woman began meeting those emotional needs.

Workaholic tendencies. This trait is common for many husbands in troubled marriages. They are driven to excel at the workplace; their marriage and home life suffer as a result. "I threw myself into my job," said one husband. "It was my escape. I could go to the office and forget everything that was happening at home. Unfortunately, at four o'clock, I had to face reality again." This escapism by the husband can set up an emotional neediness in the wife, making her vulnerable to inappropriate relationships with other women.

Suppressed emotions. Men generally have more difficulty identifying and expressing their emotions than women. The husband with a gay wife may have built up a huge load of anger, resentment, fear and hurt. Yet he does not know how to express these feelings in a healthy way. The feelings build up inside and come out in indirect and damaging ways.

Ignorance of the wife's emotions. Often these husbands do not understand the extent of their wife's emotional needs. They have little time for pondering such "female" qualities. They focus on sex, rather than seeking to understand and meet underlying emotional needs for romance and affection.

Some wives have never had a lesbian experience, but due to past hurts, they are already struggling with a mistrust or fear of men. A woman's disappointment in her husband's ability to meet her overwhelming needs for emotional intimacy leaves her hurt and detached from him. He may play into this detachment by becoming exasperated with her unrealistic demands. So his wife unknowingly becomes a prime target for a lesbian relationship.

Men who sense these dynamics in their marriage should take serious note. A wise husband will not ignore these signs or dismiss them as PMS (premenstrual syndrome) symptoms. Yes, it's unrealistic to expect that a man can meet all these deep needs in a victimized woman. But she needs help, and a wise husband will help her find the necessary resources to bring healing.

More than one husband has breathed a sigh of relief when his wife has made a new female friend who provides close companionship. Now the pressure is off him to meet all those mysterious emotional needs that he doesn't understand. Later, when it's too late, the husband may discover that his wife's new friend has taken a much greater role in her life than he ever imagined.

Meeting Emotional Needs

Many of the principles found throughout this chapter, even though heavily geared to wives with a gay husband, also apply to a husband dealing with a lesbian wife. Her issues usually predated your wedding.

Typically, the adult lesbian has been deeply wounded by men, usually through sexual and emotional abuse. If same-sex emotional deprivation also occurred, a woman can be drawn into lesbian relationships.

These are issues which a husband did not cause and cannot solve. But he can learn to give *emotional* support to his wife during her time of counseling. Here are some pointers.

Verbalize your support. Tell your wife—frequently—how much you love her, need her and want to support her through this difficult time. If you have never been able to verbalize your feelings in this way, be willing to take up this challenge one step at a time. Perhaps you would be more comfortable telling her in writing. Pick up a special card or write a brief affectionate note. Seek input from other men on ways that they have been able to offer emotional support to their wives.

Become educated about your wife's emotional needs. Husbands can flounder in this area. One man confessed, "When my wife used to become emotional, I tried to explain logically how she should respond—which only made her angry at me. Since then, I have learned that my 'logic' isn't the answer. I need to listen and support her in the midst of the troubling situation."

There are a wealth of books on all aspects of marriage, including the specific issue of a woman's emotions. Many other men have gone through situations similar to the territory through which you are moving. Read their insights and shorten your learning curve.[12]

Learn the basics about lesbianism. There are also outstanding resources to help a husband understand why his wife was vulnerable to lesbianism in the first place. This knowledge will help a husband know how to pray better for his wife and how to avoid setting her up for future temptations.

Provide physical affection (not just sex). A woman is not primarily drawn into a lesbian affair for the sex. Some lesbians stay for years in a relationship which has ceased to include sex at all. Usually a woman is hooked by the emotional intimacy, then the physical affection (which is different from sex). Physical affection includes touching, hugging, sitting close and other acts of support.

If your wife was a victim of sexual abuse, you may need to abstain from sex altogether for a period of time while she deals with this traumatic part of her past (there is more specific information on this subject in chapter six).

Offering Support to a Struggling Spouse

You may be reading this chapter because you are committed to your marriage and your spouse appears to be making efforts to overcome this issue. If this is the case, how can you be the best possible support for your spouse?

Most important, stay in prayer. Bathe this situation in prayer, because great spiritual warfare is occurring in your spouse's life. Satan is called "the murderer" (John 8:44), and he will kill your marriage if at all possible. The Bible teaches that Satan blinds the mind of those he attacks (2 Corinthians 4:4), so pray that the truth about homosexuality will become evident in your spouse's life. Pray that your partner will see the underlying emotional needs that are seeking fulfillment. Pray that your spouse will see the destructive impact of homosexual sin on your life and your children's lives. Then give verbal encouragement by telling your spouse that you are praying about the situation.

Keep your own spiritual life in order. This will empower your influence and your prayers as well. In Job 22:30, the Amplified Bible says, "He will even deliver the one for whom you intercede who is not innocent, yes, he will be delivered through the cleanness of your hands." When you enter into a close communion with God, he can give you special insight into your spouse's situation. This period of your life can become a time of major spiritual growth.

Maintain your own interests and relationships. Don't let homosexuality become the theme of your existence, even though it may be a major focus for your spouse right now. Spend some time on your own friendships, hobbies and other interests. You need time away from the problems at home.

Don't become a parent to your spouse. It's tempting to nag and cajole. Wives, being a "mother" to your husband won't help his situation in the long run. And don't seek to become your spouse's main source of ac countability. The details of his or her sin—either past or present—can be shared with a trusted same-sex counselor. You have a right to know in general how your spouse is doing, but spare yourself the minute details of each temptation. It's not fair to you, and it's not helpful to your spouse.

Be willing to work on your issues too. Ouch! Marriage problems are rarely all one partner's responsibility. The pathway out of this dark place in your marriage is a mutual journey. Part of your prayer time should include self-examination so that you can face issues of your own that God brings up in your life.

Seek your own source of accountability. Many spouses are helped by finding their own support group for encouragement. Some of the ex-gay ministries have special services and groups for spouses. Keep in mind that there are specialized resources for you too (see the appendices in this book).

God desires the best for you. He also desires the best for your spouse. With his help, your marriage may survive this test and come out even stronger in the end.

That's the testimony of Lisa Stricker, whose husband confessed his homosexual involvement just weeks after their tenth wedding anniversary. Although George was repentant, Lisa went through months of depression, anger, frustration and hurt. Finally she couldn't stand the pressure inside, and she screamed her true feelings out to the Lord. "God, why? I'm so angry! I hate what he did to me!"

Lisa recalls, "I gave full vent to every feeling I'd been suppressing for so long. I let it all out instead of holding it in and being strong. It was at that point of need that I could receive comfort from my heavenly Father." Not long later, her crippling depression left—never to return. Lisa still had a long journey ahead of her, but the battle with depression was over.

"That was five years ago," Lisa continues. "God has moved us forward with lightning speed. My relationship with the Lord has only grown more intimate. Now I know that only my heavenly Father can give me the kind of love that satisfies that deep place of need in my heart. Jesus comforted and healed the pain from my husband's betrayal and took away all of my doubt, fear and anger. My Source has shifted from a fallible human to the infallible Father who will never forsake me."

Lisa concludes, "God stepped in and changed our lives forever. I never would have chosen the path that God has put me on. But today I wouldn't change it, even if I could."[13]

10
When
a Friend Says,
"I'm Gay"

Y

ou may be reading this book because you have a friend or acquaintance who you suspect or know is gay. Maybe the person is a relative, someone you see occasionally at family gatherings. Or perhaps the person is a neighbor, fellow student or coworker. In this chapter we will examine specific strategies on how to effectively reach out to these friends.

First we'll look at general principles of friendships which are not romantic. In the next chapter, we'll examine the situation where a person is involved romantically—either dating or engaged—with a person who confesses a homosexual struggle.

When You Don't Really Know

If you have a strong suspicion that friends are lesbian or gay but the subject has never come up, it's important that you do not label them by asking if they are homosexual. They may never have thought about it, and raising the question can make them begin to question their identity.

Or it may strengthen a latent fear they already have within themselves.

The belief "Once gay, always gay" is very strong in our culture. We have seen many men go into a gay lifestyle because of something as simple as a same-sex dream that went unchecked. They gave in to fear and then became curious about homosexuality. "I tried it once just to prove that I wasn't gay," explained one man who was subsequently drawn into many same-sex encounters.

World-renowned sex researchers Masters and Johnson found that the fourth most prevalent fantasy of "straight" men was homosexual encounters.[1] And in our society those who have a gay thought or desire are urged to accept their homosexuality.

But this reasoning runs exactly opposite to the Bible. All of us have fleshly desires which war against the soul (Romans 7:23). Taking on the gay identity is a major step into spiritual deception. All of us have areas of temptation, but our identity as Christians is centered in Christ, not in our fleshly struggles.

How can we help a friend if we suspect that he or she has this problem?

Work on deepening your friendship. Become a "safe" person with whom that man or woman can be honest. Sexuality is an intimate area of life, and it takes time to deepen a friendship to the level where such private subjects can be discussed openly. Make an effort to become a reliable, consistent friend.

Pray for your friendship. Even if the other person's problem is not homosexuality, you may be discerning a struggle which needs prayer. Ask the Lord to show you how to be a better friend and find specific ways to support this person.

Be open about your own struggles. Be willing to risk your reputation. If you are hoping that your friend will open up at a deep level, you can reach that level of communication by opening up first.

Often as Christians we feel that people expect us to be perfect, and we try hard to live up to that false image. What a mistake! We end up erecting false barriers because others with deep life struggles feel that we could never understand them. But our honesty opens the door for others to share openly with us. We begin to connect with each other in a way that is genuine and life-changing.

Mention homosexuality in a neutral context. Those who struggle with this issue constantly have their "radar" on full alert, picking up the attitudes of those around them in regard to this subject. They remember unkind remarks and cutting jokes about gays for months or even years.

A married pastor who struggles with homosexual temptation relates, "Recently the music minister at my church made some comment to another man and held out his hand in the stereotypical limp-wristed fashion. They both laughed, and I hurt inside. I consider myself a fairly masculine male. I play sports, work on cars and do house repairs. Yet I would never feel comfortable going to these two men in a time of need. They wouldn't understand me."[2] Be careful not to offend those who may secretly struggle in this area. As Christians we are called to love others, not condemn them.

People who profess Christianity but who hold up signs at the gay parades like "AIDS is the cure for homosexuality" are not responding in true Christlike love. Sometimes our judgmental attitude is less obvious. We may know better than to make a remark such as "Get a load of those two faggots across the street!" But we may still project an attitude of hostility when we meet someone who has outward signs of being gay.

If you struggle with being judgmental (and all of us do at times), be honest with God. Become educated on the subject of homosexuality. As you gain understanding of the early life traumas which often lead to homosexual behavior, you will gain compassion for those caught in its trap.

Non-Christian Friends

You may have no doubt that your friend *is* gay or lesbian. This person has talked about it with you or others. Now what?

The authors of this book are often asked, "How do you share Christ with a homosexual?" Our response: "The same way you share him with anyone else!" We make a mistake when we imagine that the person dealing with homosexuality needs to be approached with the claims of the gospel in some totally unique way.

When we become aware of something "different" about other people, we can become uncomfortable and overly focused on that one area of their life. It's like talking to a man with a crooked nose; as much as we try, we cannot keep from looking at his nose! The same principle tends to operate when we are talking to homosexuals: we become consumed with their sexuality, forgetting that there are many other aspects of their lives which have nothing to do with same-sex inclinations.

Ideally, sharing the claims of the gospel occurs in the context of an ongoing friendship. John Paulk likes to tell the story of his conversion. John was heavily involved in "drag" culture, performing on stage and entering numerous beauty contests as a female impersonator. He seemed an unlikely candidate for becoming a conservative Christian.

John worked as manager of an instant-copy center on his college campus. On a regular basis the man who led one of the campus Christian fellowships would bring in small copying jobs. John can remember what an impression this man made on him: "Tom always seemed so interested in *me* as an individual. He treated me differently from any of my other customers. I found myself looking forward to talking with him when he came in, even though I knew he led a Christian group on campus."

After several months of building a friendship, Tom asked if he could visit John at home. *Uh-oh, he's going to talk to me about God,* John thought. But he was so curious that he agreed. Tom visited his apartment and began talking about Jesus Christ.

After about twenty minutes John stopped him. "I know all about the gospel," he said. "I used to go to church when I was fifteen. But I was born gay, so forget it!"

"No, you weren't," Tom answered and read from the first chapter of Genesis: "And God created man . . . male and female. . . . God saw all that he had made, and it was very good." That afternoon, after Tom showed him additional Bible passages, John became convinced that homosexuality was not something he was born with—or something that he had to stay in.

That week he dug out his Bible and started to read it again. After wrestling with the decision for days, he knelt down beside his bed. "God," he prayed, "I don't know how to get out of homosexuality, but I will follow you. No matter how difficult it gets, I'll never turn away from you again."

Since that day in February 1987, John's life has changed dramatically. After several years of involvement in an ex-gay ministry in California, he fell in love with a woman in his church. He and his wife, a former lesbian, were married in July 1992 and now are involved in an ex-gay ministry in Portland, Oregon. John has had numerous opportunities to share his story with radio and television audiences across the country, giving hope about the reality of change that is possible through Jesus Christ.[3]

Don't make homosexuality the primary point of your evangelistic conversations, but don't avoid the subject if it comes up. Most non-Christians know that the traditional biblical viewpoint condemns homosexual behavior. Gently explain that the Bible condemns *all* sexual behavior outside of heterosexual marriage, so the same standard applies to all single people, no matter to whom they are sexually attracted. If you're single, it can be helpful to share how God is helping you live up to this standard. If you're married, talk about the inappropriate attractions you've had to deal with—before and after your wedding day. Emphasize that God empowers us to obey him; we don't attain sexual purity on our own strength. If we desire to please the Lord, he will help us in our weakness (2 Corinthians 12:9-10).

Be very clear that God condemns homosexual behavior—but not homosexuals as people. A homosexual may ask, "Does God hate me?" The answer is no. The Bible is clear that God has a deep love for everyone (John 3:16; Romans 5:8). It's because of his love that he warns against sexual behavior which he knows will harm us.

If the subject of homosexuality does keep coming up, a helpful book to give your friend is *You Don't Have to Be Gay* by Jeff Konrad (see appendix A for details). This book consists of a series of letters between a former homosexual and his gay friend who is seeking the truth. They discuss roots and causes of homosexuality, loneliness, the dynamics of gay relationships and a multitude of other issues that your friend will probably be wondering about. The book is also excellent study material for you. Seeing how Jeff handled these topics will give you lots of ideas on how to discuss them with your friend. About halfway through the book Jeff's friend becomes a Christian, and the remainder shows how you can encourage a new believer who is dealing with homosexual issues.

Christian Friends Involved in Homosexuality

What about friends who profess to be Christian but who are actively involved in lesbianism or homosexuality—and defending their moral choices? Some of them may have once been part of your church, attempting to walk away from illicit same-sex relationships. But they grew tired of resisting the pull toward homosexual or lesbian behavior, and now they have adopted a pro-gay theology. How should you respond?

Treat them as you would a heterosexual friend who is pursuing sex outside of marriage. You may know other friends from church who have discarded conservative moral values and now are pursuing sinful behaviors. If so, how do you relate to them? What is an appropriate response?

In determining how to react, we have to take several factors into consideration. As believers, we want our relationship with Jesus Christ to impact others who have not yet discovered his reality in their lives. Yet we worry about being too tolerant of sinful behavior in others. There are several possible responses. Some people totally ignore another person's morality. *Their private behavior is none of my business,* they reason. On the surface, this may seem like the most "loving" approach—but is it biblical? We think not. The Bible discusses our private behavior and even our thoughts at great length. It doesn't hesitate to give moral standards that we are commanded to obey. The apostle Paul commands Christians to "flee from sexual immorality" (1 Corinthians 6:18). The writers of the Scriptures did not hesitate to detail the moral failures of biblical figures and discuss how their behavior brought grief to God's heart. God loves us, but he does not overlook our moral choices.

Another possible reaction is shunning a Christian involved in homosexuality or lesbianism. Those who act this way usually quote such Scriptures as "Come out from them and be separate, says the Lord" (2 Corinthians 6:17) and Paul's instruction, "You must not associate with anyone who calls himself a brother but is sexually immoral" (1 Corinthians 5:11). Paul adds, "With such a man do not even eat." How do these verses apply to this situation?

Some Christians take these passages at face value—and avoid even speaking to a person who professes Christianity yet indulges in homosexual acts. To have an ongoing relationship of any kind, they reason, would imply approval of the friend's immorality. And other weaker Christians who see our friendship may wrongly think that homosexuality must be OK. Will our actions cause others in the church to "stumble" into this behavior themselves?

Social isolation, however, seems to contradict Jesus' behavior. He didn't shun people around him who lived contrary to his standards. He reached out to them—but confronted them about their behavior. "Neither do I condemn you," he told one adulterous woman. "Go now and leave your life of sin" (John 8:11). He attended social events with "sinners," much to the disdain of the Pharisees (Matthew 9:11).

Other Christians interpret Paul's instructions to mean "Do not have *ongoing* fellowship with someone who is sexually immoral." In the light of this interpretation, a periodic phone call is different from ongoing, regular communication. The main motive of the relationship is to be a redemptive influence, reminding that person of the truth and attempting to lead them to a place of repentance regarding their immoral behavior.

Here's how one man, Rob, found himself working through this situation. "James and I were close friends at one time. He had been in the church for several years when I first came, and he reached out to me with genuine friendship that was really encouraging. Soon we were getting together for hiking or other activities several times a month." When James disclosed his ongoing homosexual struggles, Rob found the fact surprising, but it didn't change his interest in their friendship.

About two years later James decided to get an HIV test. He had fallen periodically into homosexual behavior and knew that he was at risk. His AIDS test came back positive. Over the next few months he struggled with deep anger and disappointment. Why had God allowed him to get infected? He was making concerted efforts to stop his immoral behavior and was eagerly pursuing a closer relationship with the Lord. He had even served overseas for a one-year short-term missions project. And now this!

James soon left the church and began spending time on weekends at gay bars in a nearby city. Months later, he called Rob and announced that he had "married" his male roommate in a gay church ceremony.

Rob was in a quandary. He had enjoyed a close friendship with James but didn't agree with his homosexual involvement. Should he continue to see James or cut off the relationship? "I decided to back away somewhat," Rob explained. "If James would call, I'd certainly talk with him. However, I tried to focus our conversation on the positive things that God was doing in my life—the same kinds of discussions that we had enjoyed in the past."

Rob found that the "glue" of their relationship—their mutual faith—had been disrupted. Suddenly a major disagreement hung over the relationship, and the dynamic of their friendship changed. "I know we both felt it," Rob says. "James knew I strongly disagreed with his active homosexual involvement. And I noticed that as he got pulled more and more into friendships with gay men, he lost interest in the spiritual things that our friendship had focused on in the past."

As James began exploring various New Age religions, their friendship became more distant. But Rob always tried to leave the door open for future communication. "I never wanted to close the door totally on the relationship. I kept praying that one day James would become dissatisfied with the gay life and would turn back to the common faith we had previously shared." James waited until the final weeks of his life to abandon his New Age beliefs and reclaim Christianity. However, he never did renounce homosexuality.

Even so, Rob was able to see James several times just prior to his death. They talked about eternity, and James said he was ready to meet the

Lord. They prayed together, and James expressed deep appreciation for Rob's visits. "When the big crisis came," Rob said, "most of James's gay friends disappeared. It's almost like they couldn't face this last chapter of death and dying in his life. But I had the Lord to help me. I could be there for James. I had earned the right to speak into his life at the end because I had maintained the relationship." When Rob saw James for the final time, he was slipping into unconsciousness. Within several days James was dead.

Rob says that seeking to maintain balance in such a relationship is difficult, and it's something that should be prayed about regularly. "I think there is a fine line between staying in touch for the sake of being a witness and compromising by maintaining the friendship as if you're in agreement with that person's behavior. I'm glad that several of us from church stayed in periodic contact with James, as I believe it paved the way for him to return to Christ in his final days. But at the same time, I couldn't remain in a close friendship with him and pretend that nothing was wrong with his homosexual relationships. It wasn't easy or always clear to me, but I tried to maintain a balance. I think God honored my efforts."

What's Your Focus in the Friendship?

Rob says that one important question helped him evaluate his relationship with James: *What is the spiritual impact of this relationship?* Rob tried to discern the results of their times together. Was their interaction pushing him away from Christ—or pulling James toward Christ? Quite frankly, sometimes it wasn't easy to tell. One night James wanted to talk about how wonderful it was to finally engage in gay sex after repressing his feelings for many years. He wasn't open to considering what the Bible had to say about sex before marriage—whether with a same-sex or opposite-sex partner. Rob went home feeling like the evening had been a waste of time.

Another night, James seemed more reflective than usual. He had "married" his lover, and they had entered into a lifelong relationship— only to find themselves splitting up seven months later because they couldn't agree on which part of the city to live in. Rob found that James was much more open to talking about spiritual things that night, including an evaluation of whether homosexual relationships were really God's best for us.

Rob didn't hesitate to seek advice from his other friends and church leaders on how to best spend his time with James. Although he probably made some mistakes, Rob felt satisfied that he had played a significant role in James's life—with eternal consequences. There are no hard-and-fast rules for this type of situation. Pray for God's guidance, as Rob did. And pray that you will have positive spiritual input into your friend's life.

One woman observes, "When I run into someone who has been part of our church and I know they have left the Lord, we usually have a warm interchange. These men and women are dear to me. Several of them are involved in immoral relationships, but usually I don't say anything about their lifestyle choices. I just pray that seeing me and sensing my love will be a reminder of good things they have left behind."

If your friend is open to discussing the biblical perspective on homosexuality, we recommend that you become acquainted with the principles behind pro-gay theology. For a quick "crash course" on the basics, we recommend appendix A in the back of *Coming Out of Homosexuality* by Bob Davies and Lori Rentzel (InterVarsity Press, 1993). For a more in-depth treatment—and a book which would be excellent to share with any active gay or lesbian friend who claims to be a Christian—we recommend *Straight & Narrow?* by Thomas Schmidt (InterVarsity Press, 1995).

As your friendship progresses, you may be faced with many of the same questions that parents ask about their gay children: What about inviting your friend's lover to dinner? What boundaries should you place on seeing them together? and so on. For further guidance on these types of situations, you can turn to the relevant sections of chapter eight.

Your friend may reach the point where he or she wants help in dealing with homosexuality. Do you have anything to offer, even though you have never struggled with this issue? Certainly! But depending on the genders of you and your friend, your friendship has special opportunities and also potential problems.[4]

For Women Only: Helping a Female Friend Who Is Struggling
Being accepted by a female straight friend is very healing for an ex-gay woman. Many lesbians are struggling with rejection issues at the deep level of their sexual identity or sense of womanhood. Typically, these women feel an intense need for same-sex approval and emotional bonding with other women. You can provide a godly example of a nonsexual friendship.

Many years ago while my husband was out of town, I spent a Saturday night at Patty's house so we could attend her church together the next morning. I was a little uncomfortable because Patty was fairly new out of the lesbian life, but soon we were chatting together and having a great time.

As we were getting ready for church the next morning, I noticed that although Patty was very attractive, she could benefit from a little blush and lipstick. But did I dare suggest it? Would she think I was being critical of her looks, or trying to change her in an outward, artificial way? After a minute's thought, I realized that I would share makeup tips with other friends, so why not Patty too? "Do you want to try this light lipstick?" I asked, and she was eager to try it. She liked the result, and we went off to church.

The next time I saw her, she couldn't wait to show me her new look. Patty had visited a makeup counter at a department store and looked great. She told me that she had never had an opportunity to experiment with makeup as a teenager and that she was now enjoying the freedom to experiment. Just a little encouragement at the right time can have quite an impact in your friend's life.

You can help your friend break old patterns of relating, such as manipulation, self-pity and selfish emotional demands, by remaining constant and faithful. You can also hold her accountable for her end of the relationship, challenging her to develop mutuality rather than dependency.

Special Cautions
While a lot of good can come of your friendship, be aware of possible

pitfalls. Some "straight" women fall into a lesbian relationship with an-other woman seeking help. Even women with no previous history of lesbianism—but who are emotionally needy—have experienced strong lesbian feelings in these types of friendships.

We cannot be naive in this regard. Same-sex attraction between wom-en is based on a genuine God-given need for intimacy that has been twisted. We all have a need for love. God made us social beings, and it's common for women to find a deep satisfaction in forming significant friendships with other women. If these same-sex needs are currently unmet, even "straight" women can find themselves drawn into inappro-priate relationships.

The fall into lesbianism can be *very* subtle, starting with an exagger-ated emotional need to be with the other person. One of the major danger signs that this relationship has taken a bad turn is the presence of jealousy and possessiveness. Your lesbian friend feels insecure, and you increasingly need to reassure her of your commitment to the friend-ship. Some feelings of jealousy are common. But when they begin to control the relationship, it's time for an evaluation, perhaps with the help of a counselor or spiritual adviser.

Another danger sign is feeling overly responsible for your friend's feelings. You may begin to be consumed with making your friend happy, taking on a responsibility that God never gave you. Overall, this relation-ship becomes hard work as you do more and more to assure your friend of your unconditional love.

Beware of the "just us" mentality. A healthy friendship is not exclusive. It welcomes others into its company. And a healthy relationship is flex-ible. If a luncheon date or night out together is canceled now and then, it's disappointing but not crushing. The person who cancels should not be made to feel guilty. Emotionally dependent relationships are marked by a clinging possessiveness, not wanting to let go at any time, even though the reasons for being apart are fully understandable.

Make sure that you maintain other close friendships. They are an important safeguard to keep your relationships in balance. Encourage your friend to pursue other friendships too. Don't believe for one mo-

ment that you are the only one who can *really* help her! It will help to
spend time with your friend in a group setting. Invite others to lunch
with the two of you. Get involved in church groups where you interact
with others. These safeguards will help avoid the exclusivity which can
lead to an emotional dependency.

Women coming from a lesbian background may have fallen into overly dependent relationships because they don't know proper boundaries
in a healthy friendship. I was counseling Martha one day on this subject.
She had phoned and asked me out to lunch. Soon we were sitting at an
outside restaurant on a beautiful sunny day.

Martha seemed somewhat preoccupied as we started our meal. I asked
her what was wrong, and she looked up at me. "Anita," she asked, "do
you think two greeting cards and a phone call are too much in one
week?" I started laughing—realizing that I tended to have the same
problem in my relationships—and she joined in. Then her face grew
sober again. "You know . . . with Sarah. I value our relationship, but I
don't know what is normal."

Martha and Sarah were both coming out of a lesbian past, and they
had become emotionally dependent on each other during the past year.
Now they were trying to find a balance in their relationship. I was encouraged that Martha could be so vulnerable with me, and I weighed my
words carefully. "Yes, I think that two cards and a phone call are a little
excessive in one week, unless there is a special reason for it." She didn't
look too pleased at my response.

I continued, "Think about your relationship with Betty from church.
You two are close, aren't you?" When she quickly agreed, I asked, "How
much contact do you have with her in a week?"

Martha thought a moment before answering. "I guess we talk about
once a week, and I send her a card on special occasions or if she needs
a little extra encouragement." She couldn't hide her disappointment as
she asked, "I guess that's what is normal for friends?" I nodded, and then
we both smiled. Even though it was hard, Martha was learning healthy
patterns in relating to other women. She persevered in the following
months, continuing to interact in a healthy way with Sarah. Today, over

five years later, they live in different parts of the country but have a good friendship and still keep in touch periodically.

For Men Only: Helping a Guy Who Is Struggling

Most male homosexuals have suffered a deprivation of same-sex bonding in their early lives. They are eager to have approval from other men. So you have a special opportunity to build confidence in your friend's life through your acceptance of him as another man. You can help him by being vulnerable about your own life, discussing your weaknesses and fears as well as your strengths. This openness helps him realize that many of his problems are the same as any man's. Not all his struggles are "gay" issues.

Become a prayer partner and invite mutual accountability. Your friend needs someone to offer him support during times of sexual temptation. If you have had problems with heterosexual immorality in the past, you have much to offer your friend in terms of practical insights into the battle against lust. Most men struggle with visual temptation. Whatever spiritual strategies have worked for you will also be effective against your friend's homosexual lust. Enlist his prayer support in your areas of weakness too.

Be willing to hear some of the nitty-gritty details of your friend's struggles. (For example, he shouldn't have to be afraid to say the word *masturbation* in your presence.) But there is a difference between being honest and being graphic. Details of his past sexual exploits are unnecessary. He can be informative without burdening you with inappropriate details of specific people, places and sexual acts.

You will also have to be honest in letting him know how much specific detail you can handle about his current struggles. If knowing his attraction to a mutual friend is too burdensome for you, he needs to know that. He can keep you abreast of his struggles without giving specific names. He needs to know your limits in other areas too, so that he does not cause you to sin by stirring up sexual fantasies in your own mind.

You may be surprised to discover how many current or past struggles in your life match those of your friend. His homosexuality is not really a sexual problem; it's merely the surface symptom of deeper root issues which need healing. The roots of homosexuality are mainly emotional and center on issues like envy *(I'm not as masculine/secure/aggressive as other men)*, rejection *(I've never felt really loved)*, loneliness *(nobody would love me if they knew the real me)* and deception *(I'll never amount to anything)*. Do any of these sound familiar? Of course they do—many of these feelings and thoughts plague all of us to varying degrees. So you can share with your friend that these issues are not "gay," they are universal. And you can share how God has helped you deal with comparable struggles in your own life.

Your friend may become too dependent on you. He may become too demanding of your time. In a few cases, he may even confess sexual attraction toward you or feelings of "falling in love" with you. Lots of straight men run for the hills at this point, which confirms to your friend that he's a complete failure and will never form a healthy friendship.

Running away is not God's best solution to this awkward situation. This is an important time in your relationship and an opportunity for you to make right decisions which will impact your friend's life in a major way. The answer is not to flee but to establish appropriate boundaries. Let's look at some specific guidelines.

First of all, if a dependency develops, don't ignore the signals that he is becoming demanding of you. You need to stand firm and gently confront him. You might say something like this: "Chuck, I can't be there for you all the time. Only God can. I am still your friend, but I feel that you are becoming too dependent on our friendship." So be honest in your communication with him; don't dodge the issue in the hope that the emotional dependency will somehow resolve itself on its own.

Second, your friend may need some basic education about the dynamics of male relationships in our culture. In a nutshell, men tend to bond in groups while doing activities together. Your friend may have unrealistic expectations about an intense one-on-one friendship with you. Perhaps this is the pattern he experienced in gay relationships, but that is atypical in heterosexual culture. He needs to understand that reality so he will not feel rejected when you begin inviting him along on group activities, rather than just spending time alone with him.

The safety of a group dynamic is especially important if he is being pulled sexually or emotionally toward you in wrong ways. He needs to be drawn into other male-male relationships, and you might have to set some clear boundaries on the time you spend with him. Don't retreat entirely, but seek balance in your friendship by limiting your time alone with him. Welcome him into group activities by inviting him along when you and your buddies attend a ball game, concert or church retreat. You can become his bridge to forming significant relationships with other straight men.

Finally, don't push your friend into premature dating. This may seem like a logical answer to his friendship needs, but this is the last thing he needs if he's just beginning the process of emotional healing. Until he becomes secure in his masculinity through forming right relationships with other men, he is not ready to tackle an opposite-sex romance.

For Men: How to Help a Woman Friend

Women who struggle with same-sex attractions often have a distorted view of men. Your friendship can be very healing in this regard. Show her respect, and let her get to know you as a brother. She needs to know that you are not expecting anything romantic or sexual from this relationship.

In our experience, the vast majority of women dealing with lesbianism have been sexually abused. Often they have a fear and even hatred of men because of deep emotional wounding. Your friend may have many fears lurking behind her friendly façade.

Give her time to establish trust in your relationship. One woman declined a ride home after Bible study because she would be alone with a man she didn't know well. Unknown to him, she had been raped as a teen. Respect her boundaries, and don't get offended if she says no to what you consider a kind offer.

Similarly, because many ex-gay women are dealing with abuse issues, be sensitive to her body cues regarding affection. Even if you are in a church where hugging is common, your friend may not appreciate your taking the initiative in expressing such familiarity with her. Watch how she interacts with other men in the church for guidance on how to relate with her.

Lesbians often struggle with control. They tend to dominate in order to avoid "losing control" and therefore risk being victimized again. Equality is the key to a comfortable relationship in this situation.

It may be helpful to her if you avoid a strictly "buddy" relationship. Lesbians are often comfortable relating to men in this fashion, but your friend is seeking to overcome past patterns. This doesn't mean that you should express false romantic feelings, but remind yourself and her from time to time that she is a female and treat her with a bit of extra courtesy.

Beware of premature romantic involvement if your friend is just beginning the process of overcoming her lesbian background. Sometimes a woman will become emotionally entangled with a male friend who seems "safe." If you see this occurring, don't pull away totally but seek to establish healthy boundaries in the relationship. You may want to become accountable to a mature Christian friend.

It's possible that you will feel romantically or sexually attracted to your friend. If she is just beginning her healing process, assume that she is *not* at all interested. In fact, your attractions could be her greatest nightmare come true. It's nothing personal, just that you are male. If she's been abused by men, she has struggled for years with thoughts like *I'll never trust a man again* and *Men are only interested in one thing.* Don't confirm those messages. She may have her guard down. You are a Christian and a "safe" friend. If you begin to pursue a premature romance, the relationship will quickly crumble when she realizes what is occurring. And her healing process will be badly derailed. Your friend can never enter into a successful heterosexual romance until she has resolved her lesbian issues. Both of you will be badly wounded if you enter into a premature emotional involvement.

For Women: How to Help a Male Friend

It's common for men struggling with homosexual issues to confess their secret to a woman. Often these men have had a closer relationship with their mother than with their dad, so they find it easy to confide in a female friend.

Seek to maintain the relationship as equals; resist the tendency to become a rescuer or substitute parent figure. Your friend needs to grow up. Many male homosexuals resist facing the realities of adult manhood. Don't keep him in a "little boy" syndrome by taking responsibility for his life.

Don't shield him from the consequences of his bad choices. Many gay men are masters at blame-shifting; their problems are the fault of everyone else but themselves. Don't allow your friend to manipulate you into thinking that he is always the victim and you need to rescue him.

Encourage his friendships with other men. This is one of the most important things you can do. Many gay men felt separated from other men as they grew up; they fear other men and feel insecure around them. They have attempted to bond with men through sexual relationships. Now they must learn to bond emotionally through appropriate activities.

If you are a sports enthusiast, you may find that you have something to teach your friend that he missed out on as a kid. If your friend is a novice at tennis but you're accomplished, offer to give him a few lessons. He will find it much less threatening to learn from you than from another man. (Vast numbers of gays have been ridiculed in their youth by male peers for being athletically challenged!) Perhaps you and your friend can invite along other people from church to enjoy a hike or ball game with you. Including others in your activities can be a good safeguard for you too.

Too often, a woman in this type of relationship will begin to become romantically inclined toward the man. She begins to hope that this platonic relationship could develop into a romance. Unless the man has had considerable time to move forward in his healing process, such a hope will only lead to hurt and disappointment. Typically, the ex-gay man will turn tail and run when he senses even a hint of romantic interest on your part. The relationship will quickly become strained and will very likely break apart.

So enjoy your friendship, but realize your limitations. You are a woman, and your friend will find his primary source of healing through appropriate emotional intimacy with other men. Keep your relationship with him in balance by spending quality time with other men and women, and you will be an important part of his support system in finding emotional wholeness and spiritual maturity.

11

Entering into Romantic Friendships: Concerns & Questions

*T*odd can vividly remember the night he met Sue. He was attending a new church, and it was his first time at the college and career group which met Friday nights.

"I walked into the fellowship hall. Sue was talking with several of her girlfriends. I noticed her immediately. She had long auburn hair, a sparkling laugh and an attractive figure. I was smitten with her right away."

Over the next three months, Todd saw Sue weekly at college and career meetings. She was always warm and friendly to him. One night after the meeting, he asked if she would be interested in going out for coffee. To Todd's amazement, they ended up talking for over two hours, and somehow the conversation got around to their plans for after college graduation.

Here's what Todd remembers about that night's conversation: "We began talking about our hopes for the future. We had talked about it a little bit previously, but on this night we really got into the details. We were both a little amazed to realize that we had similar goals. Above all, we both desired to put the Lord first in our lives."

Todd was aware of an emotional intensity and a growing mutual attraction. "When I got home that night, I was floating on cloud nine." The next week, Todd and Sue went out on Saturday evening for their first official date. After the movie, they went for a drive.

An Important Confession
"Todd, there's something important that I want you to know about me," Sue said as they drove down the highway. Then she described how as a child she had always felt "different." When puberty hit, she had felt confused about her lack of interest in boys. Then in high school Sue met two senior students who were known lesbians. She found herself wondering if perhaps she was gay. After several months Sue got to know these women better, and they introduced her to other students who were experimenting with lesbianism. During the rest of high school, Sue became sexually involved with three different women.

Then a man from work challenged Sue to consider Christianity. By the end of that summer, she had prayed to commit her life to Christ. She had now been a Christian about two years. "I've never been in a serious dating relationship with a guy," Sue concluded. "And I've never felt such strong feelings for a man."

During the coming months, Todd and Sue became an established couple at church. Others began affirming their relationship, especially Sue's close friends who knew of her past involvement in lesbianism. Todd was thrilled at this development in his life, even as further details unfolded about Sue's troubled childhood. Her parents had divorced when she was seven after her father committed adultery. Sue had been deeply wounded by her parents' breakup and remembered vowing never to trust a man again. She had erected thick walls around her heart to keep from being hurt again. Until Todd came along, that is.

Todd remembers some warning signs of trouble ahead in their relationship, but he ignored them. Sue was struggling with a strong emotional attachment to another woman at church. Todd knew that Sue had not been out of lesbianism for very long, but the excitement of their relationship erased his slight misgivings. "I had never been happier, especially when Sue told me she was willing to take the risk of loving me."

After nine months of dating, Todd took Sue to a well-known exclusive restaurant with a view overlooking the city. It was a perfect summer evening. A thousand lights sparkled below them as the sky darkened. After dinner Todd presented Sue with a small gift-wrapped box. Inside was an engagement ring. He held his breath as Sue read the accompanying note: "I have sought the Lord and believe he wants us to be always together. I love you. Will you marry me?"

Sue looked up, her eyes misty. "Yes, I will," she said softly. Todd could feel his own eyes flooding with tears. Later they walked arm-in-arm through the large outdoor garden of the restaurant, savoring the magic of the evening and their newfound commitment to each other. "I was never more happy," Todd said later, "and I assumed that she was feeling the same way."

Disturbing Changes

But over the next two months Todd sensed some unsettling changes in Sue. He especially remembers the weekend that they went to visit her mom and stepfather, and how cool her stepfather acted toward him. Sue cried most of the two-hour drive home, confessing to Todd that her stepfather was not a Christian and was strongly opposed to their relationship.

During the next week Sue totally withdrew emotionally, and Todd felt hurt and confused. Here's how he explained it: "That weekend was a turning point in our relationship. Due to her stepfather's rejection, all her unresolved feelings toward her real father came rushing to the surface. Our relationship began to crumble from that day on."

Todd phoned Sue, and during their conversation, Sue started weeping. It was several minutes before she could speak. "I have these feelings of aggression toward men. I don't want to be around you right now." Several days later Todd answered the doorbell. To his surprise, Sue stood on the doorstep, holding out a small box. "This is never going to work," she blurted out. "I've been thinking about this for days, and I have to tell you the truth. I'm not in love with you, and I can't marry you." She handed him the box and ran back to her car while Todd stood in his doorway, frozen with shock.

He stood in place while Sue drove off, then finally closed the door. A flood of emotions erupted inside him. "I sank down on the couch and started screaming and sobbing. It sounded like I was dying—and that's the way I felt. All I could do was pray, 'Lord, help me. I can't deal with this. Help me make sense of what is happening right now.' "

Todd later phoned Sue and tried to reason with her. "I think you do love me deep down inside, but your issues with men have come up and you can't deal with the pain. So you've shut off your heart to me."

She denied it. "You're wrong. This has nothing to do with any of those issues."

Todd tried to convince her that she was overreacting by giving up on their relationship. "If you will only face your issues with men and with your father, I'm willing to wait. I don't care how long this takes. I want to support you and see our relationship grow again in the future." But Sue refused to change her mind.

Todd knew that he was working to revive something that was already dead. "I needed to let her go. It was killing me inside, but I had to do it." He cried himself to sleep that night.

That was three years ago. Since then, Sue has moved to another part of the country. Todd is now dating another young woman from work. Periodically he hears news of Sue through mutual friends at church. She is doing well, although he does not know if she has been able to process further the issues that were raised in their relationship. "I knew after that last conversation that it was time to really let her go and move on with my life," he says. "I wish her God's very best. And despite the outcome, I have no regrets that I pursued that relationship. I learned a lot, especially the fact that I am capable of loving someone very deeply. Some of the lessons I learned are playing out in my current relationship. I'm a better person for knowing Sue."

Romantic Relationships

Todd's story is not unusual. A former homosexual or lesbian often becomes aware of deep unresolved issues in the context of pursuing a serious heterosexual romance. This is not to imply that these relationships *never* work out. On the contrary, I know many former gays and lesbians who have successfully come through a period of dating and engagement, and who are now happily married. In fact I'm married to one of them! Let me tell you a little bit about my experiences with Frank.

Our first real time together occurred in the unlikeliest place—Disneyland. I had met Frank several years before at a seminar where he was teaching. It was not love at first sight for either of us. I thought Frank was kind of dull and stuffy—an old bump on a log. He thought I was a "brassy woman." Not a promising beginning.

Then I moved to the Los Angeles area and began helping Barbara Johnson with her Spatula ministry to parents and friends with a gay loved one. She had known Frank for years and secretly decided that we should get acquainted. When he came down to Los Angeles for a speaking engagement, Barbara was supposed to take him and another visitor to Disneyland. Instead, she asked me to take them. All three of us had a great time that day. No romance was involved, but I discovered Frank's quirky, dry sense of humor. I liked it.

The next day at work I was reminded of an important experience in my life. A few years before, I had been in prayer with several other women. I had been grieving about being single, and I shed a lot of tears that day with my friends. While we were praying, I began to see a vision in my mind of the type of man that I would marry someday. I saw myself with someone involved in ministry. I knew that I could be an understanding wife to someone who might counsel with others far into the night. I also saw travel being part of the picture. A missionary? Minister? I did not know exactly why lay ahead, but I walked out of that prayer time with a release from the grief I had been carrying.

Now, after meeting Frank, I had a startling revelation. Frank Worthen was everything I had envisioned in my desire for a husband! This realization gave me chills down to my toes. But I wanted to know if this was really from the Lord; I didn't want to get into some romantic fantasy. So I prayed frequently about the whole matter and waited to see what would happen.

Soon after that, I visited Frank and his ex-gay ministry in the San Francisco Bay area. The Lord allowed me to see Frank at his worst. He was not feeling well and was quite grumpy. But as we got to know one another, I saw that we were compatible. The more time I spent around Frank's ministry and church, the more I fell in love with everything in San Rafael. When Frank drove me to the train station for my trip home, I burst into tears on the freeway, declaring my love. Poor Frank didn't know what to do (he has never liked a "tearful woman").

I needed the ten-hour train ride home to get my emotions together! So much was at stake. Never before had I felt so much at home as I did at Frank's church and ministry in San Rafael. But because of my growing feelings for Frank, I knew it wouldn't work for me to come back and work here without being married to him.

During the coming weeks, we were both praying a lot about our friendship. I wrote Frank a thank-you note and made it sound casual (even though I rewrote it four times). I phoned him once, and he was careful to say, "*We* enjoyed having you." I talked to him again later, and he was more specific: "I really enjoyed having you here, and I would love to see you before I go to Europe next month on a ministry trip." Our romance was officially *on* from that point.

Early in our courtship, Frank and I watched a video by Jack Hayford, pastor of Church on the Way in Van Nuys, California. It had some helpful counsel that we both took to heart: go slow in your expressions of physical affection. Hayford described the steps of physical intimacy, from casual hugging to sexual intercourse. He drew the line at "brother-sister" type hugs and light kisses before marriage. Anything beyond that, he said, is a prelude to full sexual intimacy and belongs in the context of marriage.

Although everyone may not agree with Hayford's presentation, it was right for Frank and me. In my previous relationships, especially before I became a Christian, I had become too physically involved with the men

I dated. I needed to slow down. Frank, on the other hand, had pursued homosexual relationships for over twenty years and had not been involved romantically with a female since his teen years. He needed freedom from the pressure of rushing into physical expressions of romantic love.

Our relationship wasn't all smooth sailing. I wondered about our fifteen-year age difference and pondered the implications of his homosexual past (Frank had been out of homosexuality for about ten years when I met him). I was somewhat bothered that Frank wasn't more physically affectionate toward me. I wondered if he was attracted to me—and whether we could satisfy each other sexually in marriage.

Later we could look back and see that God was protecting our relationship. Frank didn't need to feel sexual about me months before the wedding. God gave him those feelings just a few weeks before our wedding; after that, we had to be careful about too much touching!

On our wedding night, it was so wonderful to lie beside my husband in bed, feeling such joy and freedom inside. Because of our inappropriate sexual relationships with others in the past, we were both overwhelmed with the awareness that *there is no guilt in the Lord.* There was no shame in our physical relationship. We could enjoy each other, knowing that we had the rest of our lives to get to know each other more deeply. The Lord has continued to bless our marriage in every way, and I thank God continually for the privilege of serving beside this committed man of God.

Many Questions

Those of us who enter into a dating relationship with a former homosexual or lesbian can have many questions: "How do I know when it's time to move into a committed relationship?" "My boyfriend is still attracted to some men—should I be concerned?" "My girlfriend is very close to her best female friends—what should I do?" We'll attempt to give you some guidance, which we base on our own experiences and years of counseling with many other individuals.

How long should people be out of homosexual behavior before they begin dating? Some leaders of ex-gay ministries recommend three years. For men and women coming from a homosexual past, a lot of healing has to occur before they are ready to consider a committed heterosexual relationship. A big part of the healing comes through relationships—first, between them and God; next, between themselves and others of the same sex. Only then can they move into a serious relationship with someone of the opposite sex. In dating an ex-gay friend, it is important to ascertain how long he or she has been free from immoral behavior.

Some might wonder what we mean by "out of homosexual behavior." Does this mean full sexual contact? Or private struggles like pornography or masturbation with same-sex fantasies? There are no universal answers to these questions. We feel that any overt sexual behavior with another person to the point of sexual climax would clearly constitute "homosexual behavior." Other actions, such as looking for sexual partners in a park frequented by gays or visiting a pornographic bookstore, would be major warning signals. If these types of gay-related behaviors are occurring with some regularity in someone's life, it indicates that the person is not ready for a committed opposite-sex relationship.

We recommend that dating, *especially* when one or both of you are coming from a gay background, should occur only if you are both ready to consider marriage. If you're not ready to pursue a relationship leading to marriage with that individual, don't date. And we are opposed to "evangelistic dating"—dating someone in order to win them over to one's own religious beliefs. Many people fall into the trap of dating non-Christians, hoping to draw them into the faith. It rarely works; more often, the Christian falls in love and marries the non-Christian, despite biblical warnings to the contrary (2 Corinthians 6:14).

In our ministry, we also see individuals who begin to date a person just emerging from homosexuality (or still involved in it) with the hope that the relationship will strengthen the person's commitment to pursuing heterosexuality. Instead, though, the ex-gay often feels under such pressure due to the relationship that he or she falls back into homosexual relationships to escape the pressure of heterosexual expectations. Premature dating can actually undermine the healing process and send the person back into sexual sin.

We expose ourselves to a lot of potential heartache if we get involved in a dating relationship before the other person is ready. If your friend has been unsuccessful in establishing a track record of sexual and/or emotional celibacy for a season before entering into a dating relationship, how do you know this person can be faithful to you?

Similarly, if you have also been involved in premarital sexual activities, you need a time of obedience to God before entering a committed relationship. When people who have been sexually active outside of marriage come to the Lord, they need a time of faithfulness to Jesus, getting to know him as the "lover of their soul" before they take on another love relationship.

Evaluating the Relationship

In this chapter, we are assuming that you are involved in a romantic friendship and you wonder about the wisdom of continuing to pursue this relationship. There are some important issues for you to consider. Here are a few appropriate questions to ask the person you are dating.

"How much were (are) you involved in homosexuality?" Jill had dated Dave for several months before he told her about his homosexual past, quickly assuring her that it had been resolved a long time ago. Later she discovered the painful truth: Dave had fallen into a homosexual encounter only a few weeks before his confession. Jill felt betrayed and deceived: "It's not fair that he let me fall in love with him *before* he told me."

Many men and women are like Dave. They tell *part* of the problem in an effort to minimize their past sin. Many dating partners, like Jill, don't know what to ask or don't really want to know any more. So no questions are raised, which is a mistake. If your dating relationship is serious, it must be built on a foundation of truth. Such confidence comes only when you really know both the strengths and the weaknesses of the other person.

It's not necessary to find out exact details (dates, places, names, description of sexual acts). But it's very important to know if your friend participated in homosexual acts or only thought of them. Was your friend regularly engaged in homosexual behavior, or was it only a few experiences? Is your friend at risk for HIV? If so, was he or she tested at least six months after the last sexual involvement? How long has your friend been totally abstinent from homosexual acts?

"Are you accountable to another mature Christian in terms of your sexual struggles?" Ideally, this accountability involves a pastor, Christian counselor or another godly person who is spiritually mature and of the same sex as the ex-gay man or woman. This question also recognizes the reality that for virtually all former gays and lesbians there is some ongoing vulnerability to sexual temptation, even after they have broken off all immoral relationships and been sexually pure for a period of time.

Many former homosexuals and lesbians have not come to the place where they can tell anyone. If you are the first and only person to know their past, you have been placed in a very important position. But be aware that this person can become very close to you quickly because you share their secret. If you have a "need to be needed" in someone else's life, this aspect of the relationship will appeal to you and may pull you into a premature commitment. The fact that this person is accountable to no one else but you is a major danger sign. It shows that, in all likelihood, the homosexual problem is still unresolved and that person is *not* ready to enter a committed dating relationship with you.

"What has God done in your life since you turned away from homosexuality?" This question gets below the level of simply stopping the lesbian or gay behavior. Homosexuality is fed by underlying emotional needs. Until the issue is resolved at that deeper level, the person is not ready for marriage.

As Christians, we all have a testimony of a changed life. Asking this question gives you an opportunity to discern if this person has really experienced God's power of transformation. Does the testimony cause your heart to leap with joy at God's goodness? Or does it raise more questions than it answers? Does this person's story make you feel even less secure? If so, you know that more honest dialogue is essential before the relationship should be pursued any further.

If You're Dating an Ex-Gay Man

Women involved in a relationship with a former homosexual frequently ask, "He's still having homosexual temptations. Should I be concerned?" The answer is, It depends how he is *responding* to those temptations. All of us have temptations; usually they are connected to past sinful behaviors. The more time we stay away from that sin area by resisting temptation, the less power that area has over us.

Your friend should be doing things that draw him closer to the Lord—and away from his old sin areas. As he consistently resists gay temptations, they should lessen in frequency and intensity over time. As he seeks God's healing in the deeper areas of his life that fuel the gay temptations, he will mature emotionally and spiritually. This process involves both time and commitment on his part. If he is pursuing God with all his heart, don't be concerned about lingering sexual temptations.

But if your friend is not totally committed to emotional healing, be careful! The most common problem we see in women dating ex-gay men is entering a relationship prematurely in an attempt to solidify the man's commitment to pursuing heterosexuality. The woman leads the relationship, and the man goes along with it out of passive agreement. As the relationship deepens, the woman realizes that the man is not resolving his homosexuality as quickly as she had hoped. He is experiencing significant homosexual temptations. He may periodically fall into "fringe gay behavior" (for example: cruising, reading gay porn, phoning gay-sex lines). In some cases, the man is even committing homosexual acts with other men. If this is your situation, we strongly recommend that you sever the dating relationship. This man is not ready for a heterosexual commitment.

Another common scenario is the "we're-just-friends" type of relationship. You and your friend are spending a lot of time alone in activities which are commonly called "dating" in our culture. You go to the movies, or out to dinner, or to a sports event. Or you take an afternoon walk or stop for a cup of coffee at the mall—just the two of you. You are a couple, but you have convinced yourself that there is "nothing serious" about the relationship. When others question the relationship, you assure them that you are not dating. "We're just friends," you say casually.

We don't recommend this type of relationship. In the vast majority of cases, it ends badly. The relationship breaks apart. The woman is devastated emotionally, and the man is disillusioned about heterosexual relationships. The woman realizes, too late, that she has made a deep emotional investment in the relationship, but the man has little or no emotional investment because he is not sufficiently healed to make such a heterosexual commitment.

If You're Dating an Ex-Lesbian

Men who are dating women from a gay background have other issues of concern. Ex-gay women are less likely to enter a dating relationship prematurely. Usually their fear or distrust of men is too strong for them to even consider being alone with a man in a potentially romantic situation (as we noted earlier, the vast majority of lesbian women seeking our help have been victims of incest or rape).

It's common for ex-gay women who are entering into heterosexual dating to have been sexually abstinent for several years. Typically, however, they struggle with the emotional side of their problem. They battle to be free from too-close emotional entanglements with other women, especially "needy" women who have also been victimized. If you are dating a woman who seems to move from one overly committed female friendship to another, this is a major sign that she is not ready to pursue a serious dating relationship with you.

Carefully examine your friend's same-sex relationships. Does she tend to hang on to old friendships with lesbian women from her past? Does she spend time with a group of women (such as a women's softball team) who are predominantly gay? Is she making significant friendships with godly Christian women in her church? If meeting with the community volleyball team is more important to her than a women's Bible study group, you will want to proceed with caution.

Another danger sign is continued rejection of her femininity. We are not advocating blue eye shadow and high heels. But a woman who has found significant emotional healing is finding her body more comfortable; she is less likely to hide herself in baggy or masculine clothing.

Finally, if the woman is unwilling to bond with you on an emotional level, use caution. If you are moving into a committed relationship, there should be a growing emotional closeness and a willingness to work out situations where feelings have been hurt. In dating, for example, it's common for a man to say something that hurts a woman's feelings. Can she acknowledge these situations when they occur and work them out? Or does she deny them and pretend that "nothing is wrong"—even when it is obviously not true?

Exciting Potential

Even though we have given many warnings and danger signs, we don't want you to leave this chapter thinking that dating a former homosexual or lesbian is wrong! We know hundreds of people in this situation who have enjoyed exciting opposite-sex dating relationships. Many of them have gone on to marriage, and now they are experiencing strong marital relationships which bring an abundance of joy and deep satisfaction.

The key element of success is committing your dating relationship to the Lord and seeking his leading each step of the way. We strongly advise you to seek pastoral counseling throughout your relationship. Anyone dating a person from a homosexual background needs to have some kind of wise counsel. Be willing to hear the truth about your relationship (even when it hurts!).

Sometimes we want something so badly that we close our eyes to the truth. If you feel that you may be doing this—even just a little—we encourage you to take some time alone with God. Perhaps you can get away for a weekend to draw closer to him. Be honest. There is nothing that he doesn't already know about your relationship. Commit your way to him, and he promises to direct your steps (Psalm 37:5, 23).

12
Finding Hope Again: Life After Homosexuality

Y*ou may still be wondering, When are these authors going to give me some* guaranteed methods to get my loved one out of this terrible mess? Surely those who have ministered to family and friends for years have some secret techniques, some sure-fire ways to help you "fix" your loved one.

Unfortunately, such methods don't exist. If they did, my son would have renounced his homosexual identity by now. Still, we believe strongly that there is hope—both for your loved one and for *you* as well.

My hope is in Jesus Christ and his ability to heal all who turn to him. Each of us has areas that need to be turned over to his care. As we begin to focus on "us," God will work on our loved one. Remember my initial reaction when I found out about Tony? I determined to get his life straightened out at any cost—as soon as possible! Since then, I've talked to hundreds of parents and friends. Many of them have the same driving desire: get rid of the problem—fast.

Some of the loved ones who contact an ex-gay ministry go away frustrated when they don't find a quick-fix formula. They take away the same grief and confusion they brought with them.

Others embrace the reality that they cannot control another person's life. They come to realize that they can *influence* their gay loved one— through unconditional love, through holding on to God's truth and through consistent prayer. These family members and friends leave our ministries with a new perspective, a softened heart, even a renewed relationship with God himself.

A Difficult Balance

There are some difficult principles in this book. Realizing that we cannot directly control another adult's choices is frustrating. But it's also reality. As Christians, we want to live in hope. But we must also face the facts of real life.

Both authors are involved in ex-gay ministry, talking daily with many men and women who have had dramatic and exciting changes in overcoming their homosexual past. Regularly we receive wedding invitations, birth announcements and other tangible reminders of God's redeeming power. But we also work with parents whose children are taking their first faltering steps toward change—or who are not interested in changing at all.

All of us dream of the day we will experience the dramatic breakthrough that one mother named Mary reported to us. Since Mary's daughter, Linda, lived only fifty miles away, she came home to visit periodically. One day Linda arrived and asked her mother to sit down in the living room. "I want to talk, Mom," she began. "I suspect this is something you've been praying about, so I want you to be the first to know. I've given my roommate a month's notice to move. Mom, I want to learn to live in your world. I want to be straight."

These words sounded like the sweetest music in the world to Mary's ears. Yes, they were the answer to a thousand prayers. Can you close your eyes and think how they would sound to you? I can. It would be marvelous!

Of course Linda's desire did not whisk her into heterosexuality. Her decision was just the first step of a long journey. Over the next several years, this mother learned firsthand how to support her daughter in seeking freedom from her lesbian past.

God wants to prepare us to help our loved one through the difficult process of change. "Dealing with my homosexuality has definitely been the supreme challenge of my Christian walk," said one married man. "I know several special people—including my parents—who have prayed with me every step of the way."

If God had answered my first tearful prayers a few days after my son, Tony, admitted that he was gay, I wouldn't have had any idea how to help him. I have needed to become educated on the subject. Now, while I still pray and wait for him to seek help, I can be effective in encouraging other men and women who are overcoming their past homosexuality.

Mary, the mother whose daughter desired to change, had years of learning about overcoming difficulties in her own life. So she was able to offer practical encouragement to her daughter, although she still had much to learn along the way. "It took several months for me to realize that the change from homosexual to straight was more than a simple choice to break away from an old way of life," Mary admits.

Later, her daughter was almost overwhelmed about the future and explained her fears this way: "Mom, I stepped out on a limb and told my family that I wanted to be straight. Suddenly my whole family loved me more, accepted me and welcomed me like I'd never experienced. And now they expected something of me—like a boyfriend. They expected me to step into this unfamiliar world and be comfortable. But I'm *not* comfortable. I am ill at ease and scared to death. I don't know how to act as a 'straight' person. I've been gay for eleven years!"

Mary saw her misery but didn't know how to help her. "My daughter had made the right decision, but her life was in utter disorder as a result of that decision." Many parents see signs of hope but still feel very insecure. "What if she doesn't make it?" they ask. "What if I say or do the wrong thing?"

Here are some things Mary learned that will help you support your gay loved ones who are in the process of seeking change.

Build them up. Call attention to their good points, positive attributes, achievements, wisdom and victories on the job. In other words, be an encouraging friend (especially toward a gay son or daughter or a spouse who is struggling). Sometimes the best thing we can do is listen. Not give advice, just hear what they have to say. This will also help us know better how to pray.

Learn about homosexuality. A lack of knowledge makes it hard to help our loved ones through the emotional roller coaster that change brings. When a person has a heart attack, the doctor gives literature to the family in order to help them learn what to expect and how to aid the recovery process. When the problem is homosexuality, we should be just as prepared to help.

Give them the gift of time. Our loved ones feel pressure to meet our expectations. When people don't want to disappoint others by admitting they have failed or they are having a hard time, they may split their lives in half. In this double life, they act out a public façade but hide their private world. We can ease some of this pressure by not pushing them into situations (such as dating) that they don't feel ready to tackle. And if they pull away from us for a season, we must let them go. Our relationship may be changing, and they need time to decide how they will relate to us now.

Let go of expectations for marriage. Parents, especially mothers, generally want marriage for their children. A decision to turn from homosexuality will bring all those hopes rushing to the surface. If children get a hint of these desires, it can do a lot of damage to their healing process. We can counteract our expectations by being thankful to God for every little step forward and by focusing on the present, not on what we hope for the future.

Forgive the past. We can do a lot of damage to our loved ones by bringing up past hurts, and they may never ask our forgiveness for some of the pain they caused us. But we can still deal with the hurts in our private prayer time. "Forget the former things; do not dwell on the past. See, I am doing a new thing! Now it springs up; do you not perceive it?

I am making a way in the desert and streams in the wasteland" (Isaiah 43:18-19). Forgiving and forgetting the past paves the way to a richer future with our loved ones.

Be their prayer partner. A nonpushy spiritual influence goes a long way in people's lives. We can offer to pray about difficult situations they are facing—without being nosy about details of the hard time they are having. They will offer details if they want us to know.

Thousands of parents like Mary have seen their child escape a gay or lesbian lifestyle. But many thousands more are still waiting, sometimes very impatiently. For those still waiting, they can become prepared, so that when and if that day comes, they will be ready to offer hope and direction to their troubled child.

"I'm a Better Person"

I remember the day, long after I found out Tony was gay, that I was able to say, "Because of what happened to my son, I am a better person today." That day was a significant turning point for me. The trauma of learning about Tony's homosexuality drew me back to the Lord for strength and comfort. Before then, I didn't want to give up my life and completely depend on God. But the situation with my son made me realize my need for the Lord in a new way.

Did God cause Tony to become homosexual in order to get my attention? No. God hates sin. Tony's destructive lifestyle grieves God even more than it grieves me. But the Bible promises that "in all things God works for the good of those who love him" (Romans 8:28). In my case, I know that this situation has been used for good. Here are some specific beneficial things that have come into my life through my struggles with Tony's situation:

Faith. "Faith is being sure of what we hope for and certain of what we do not see" (Hebrews 11:1). God has been faithful to me in so many ways, and that builds my faith for the future.

Looking back, I can see how God prepared me to learn about Tony's HIV status. Frank and I had served as missionaries in Manila for one year—and it was *quite* a year. Frank had three major illnesses, our local church had no services in English, our ministry team was having strong interpersonal conflicts, and I was starting menopause! I was thousands of miles from my family and long-time friends. Out of desperation, I was forced to develop a deeper relationship with the Lord.

During that traumatic first year, I recorded in my journal two quotes from Corrie ten Boom which meant a lot to me. The first captures my dependency on God's comfort and strength:

Yesterday He helped me,

Today He did the same.

How long will this continue?

Forever, praise His name.[1]

The second quote I recorded was "In order to realize the worth of the anchor, we need to feel the stress of the storm." At the end of that year when I learned of Tony's HIV infection, it was a traumatic and stressful time. But I had already seen many examples of God's faithfulness. I love the Scripture in the Living Bible which says, "Disaster strikes like a cyclone and the wicked are whirled away. But the good man has a strong anchor" (Proverbs 10:25). Through all the storms, my anchor was holding fast. I knew it would continue to hold during the storms to come.

Hope. Today I have hope in the Lord. I know the road ahead will be rocky for me, but God will walk beside me. He promises good things for my future in Jeremiah 29:11, " 'For I know the plans I have for you,' declares the LORD, 'plans to prosper you and not to harm you, plans to give you hope and a future.' " I place my hope in him, not in my future circumstances.

Peace. God has given me a peace that does not depend on my surroundings. It's supernatural. But like everyone else, I sometimes lose it. Fears about the future threaten to overwhelm me. My greatest weapon to fight off these fears are the promises in God's Word. One of my favorites is Isaiah 54:10, " 'Though the mountains be shaken and the hills be removed, yet my unfailing love for you will not be shaken nor my covenant of peace be removed,' says the LORD, who has compassion on you." I am also grateful that I have my husband, Frank, to support me and pray for me during this time of my life. His constant love has certainly lifted me during some of my dark days.

Thankfulness. One of my most powerful tools for fighting discouragement is thanking God out loud each day. I take time to name specific things that come to mind. When I began this habit of spending a significant chunk of my quiet time speaking out thanks, God began to show me more things for which to give thanks, things that had been there all along but which I had taken for granted. Now I have eyes that see what he has done for me—it's like getting spiritual glasses! Through seeing all that he does for me, I have begun to understand just how much he loves me.

Faithfulness. Sensing God's love—and seeing it displayed in my life—leaves me sober about my need to cultivate faithfulness in my walk with him. Of course I still fall short, but I am growing in this area of my spiritual walk. First, I am faithful to communicate, spending time alone with God to talk things over with him. And by being faithful to read and study his Word, I gain understanding of his character and how he relates to his people. With my "spiritual glasses" I see things that others may miss.

The Bible is alive to me. The other day I was reading Psalms 115 and 116 in the Living Bible. How encouraging to read these verses: "Jehovah is constantly thinking about us and he will surely bless us" (115:12), and "I love the Lord because he hears my prayers and answers them. Because he bends down and listens, I will pray as long as I breathe!" (116:1-2). I love it! He is *constantly* thinking of me, and he *bends down* to listen when I talk to him. Now that's a picture of a loving Father.

Becoming an Encourager

As I have gone through the depths of the valley and come out the other side, God has shown me that now I have something precious to share. I have received comfort from him; now he can use me to share that same comfort with others. All Christians endure suffering of some kind. But God is big enough to help us endure through the heartache. As he heals our pain, he makes us an example to others of his healing power.

"But I've never been a public speaker," you might protest, "and I'll never write a book." You might be surprised—I used to say the same thing, and now I've done both! It's true that most of us will not be called to jump into a public ministry regarding this issue. But as the issue of homosexuality becomes ever more common in our society, there are an increasing number of devastated loved ones who need your encouragement. Some of them are probably right in your church. As you are willing, God will open doors of ministry to others.

We are God's best advertisements! A good sales clerk doesn't leave the prize vacuum cleaner in a packing box. She brings it out and demonstrates its features. Without a demonstration, there is little chance that someone will buy the product. God wants us to be "walking advertisements" of his character and power.

I know many parents who have said, "God, I'm willing. Use me." Maybe there were one or two small opportunities at first, but then larger opportunities came along. Some of these parents have formed support groups for other devastated families. A few have begun ministries with national and even international influence. At one time these family members and friends were broken and shattered, just as you have been. But they pursued emotional healing and spiritual growth, then offered themselves for God to use. And he *has* used them—in mighty ways.

Humor and Encouragement
"I know a little suffering is good for the soul, but someone must be trying to make a saint out of me!" jokes Barbara Johnson in *Mama, Get the Hammer!* one of her popular books of humor.[2] Barbara is a wonderful example of an "ordinary" mother who said, "Whatever, Lord!" She didn't begin writing until she was fifty years old. Seventeen years later she has sold over two million books. You may not aspire to become another Barbara Johnson, but her worldwide ministry shows what God can do with a willing heart.

Barbara's life has impacted me in major ways. When I found out about Tony, I was encouraged by reading her first book, *Where Does a Mother Go to Resign?* I learned that another Christian mother had gone through this trauma—and survived! A few years later, when I moved from Oregon to southern California to look after my invalid mother, I became better acquainted with Barbara and Spatula, her outreach to friends and families of gay men and women.³ She's been a special friend and encouragement to me ever since.

But more than just encouraging me, she has encouraged millions of hurting parents around the world through her special ministry, including her speaking presentations and bestselling books. And you know what? Barbara is not much different from any of the rest of us. But she has a great desire to help others, and an ability to be "real" in front of a large audience. Her humility makes her very believable to those who hear her. God saw her heart and gave her an international audience to hear her message of comfort, humor and hope.

One of the best lessons I've learned from Barbara is the value of laughter. There is a saying that rings true for me, "A spoonful of sugar helps the medicine go down." I have found that humor can be a real gift and has enabled me to bring some hard truths to hurting people. Humor is also helpful in our everyday life as we face great sorrows and fears.

Some people collect stamps, coins or teaspoons. Barbara collects "gloomee-busters," humorous sayings that bring her joy on the down days. Here are a few samples from her vast collection:

☐ Have you ever felt that even though you're taking things "one day at a time" . . . it's about twenty-four hours more than you can take?

☐ Don't worry about the world ending today. It's already tomorrow in Australia.

☐ When your dreams turn to dust . . . vacuum!⁴

I love Barbara's example of finding humor to help us through the hard times.

An Eye on Eternity

Ultimately, our only hope comes from an eternal perspective. Those parents, spouses and other loved ones who are at peace—even in the midst of great uncertainty and continuing questions—are those who have chosen to put their hope in God.

Chris MacKenzie has learned this lesson. In 1980 her oldest son, Damon, moved from his family home in Illinois to Florida. "Damon and I had always been close," Chris says, "so it was difficult to see him go, but I knew he had to live his own life." Several months later, Chris received a long letter from him. "I found someone that I care deeply about," he wrote, "and I'm in a relationship that is completely fulfilling." As she read further, Chris's stomach lurched, and she could hardly swallow as Damon confessed that this relationship involved another man. "I have had these strong feelings of attraction to men for as long as I can remember," he wrote, "and I've always tried to hide them." Now Damon was "coming out of the closet" and living as he believed God intended.

"I was completely devastated," says Chris. "I screamed, I ranted, I cried. I felt like I was bleeding deep inside, and there was no way to stop the gaping wound in my soul."

Does this mean I will never see Damon married with a family? Chris wondered. *Will I have to endure holidays and family dinners with some limp-wristed man looking adoringly at Damon?* She felt nauseated at the thoughts that whirled through her mind. And she worried about her younger children, who looked up to Damon. Would he influence them to become gay too?

Chris finally concluded that if she wanted any kind of relationship with Damon, she was going to have to live with this news, not condoning it, but seeing past the "gay" label to the real person.

Damon lived in another state and continued to call regularly, sharing details of his school and work. Chris still remembers those calls. "He was more loving and respectful than ever. It made me realize that he was still my same sweet son—except for this new knowledge I had about his sexual preferences."

Then a new pastor came to Chris's church, and she became more involved. "I started teaching Sunday school and began experiencing a deeper relationship with God. I recommitted my life to Christ and started trying to live for him." She became good friends with her new pastor's wife and confided in her about Damon. "She gave me needed sympathy and a good shoulder to cry on. She never condemned Damon, but suggested that we put his name on our ongoing prayer list. I had prayed for Damon in the past, but not with a deep conviction that he could change."

The women prayed for Damon. Chris also prayed for God's healing in her own life. "It's too much of a burden for me to carry around," she prayed. "God, I need you to do your work. My own efforts have been useless."

In 1991 Damon came home for a visit. During one of their talks, he told his mother that the fulfillment and happiness he had sought with other men just wasn't there anymore. He was emotionally drained and seriously considering getting help for exiting his gay lifestyle. "I was stunned and overjoyed!" says Chris. "He had been in different relationships for twelve years. Was this an answer to my prayers—finally?"

Damon had contacted Exodus International, a worldwide coalition of ministries to men and women seeking freedom from homosexuality. He planned to attend their upcoming national conference. Chris was thrilled. "I was convinced this *had* to be an answer to prayer. Not only that, but if Damon could be healed, it would be a miracle." When Damon came back from the conference, she could see an excitement, a new softness and a love for God that wasn't there before. "He had a hunger for godly things. He had recommitted his life to Christ and made a vow of celibacy. I praised God for his goodness and mercy."

The next year, Damon joined one of the Exodus ministries with a residential program for men overcoming homosexuality. Both he and his mother attended that year's Exodus conference. During the conference, Chris faced an unexpected and devastating blow. Damon confessed that he was infected with the HIV virus.

"That was probably the hardest thing I've ever had to face," Chris says. "My heart felt torn into a thousand pieces." *My son is dying!* she thought as she cried on his shoulder. Then came feelings of anger. "How could you do this? You knew AIDS was out there. Why didn't you stop when you had that first test and it came back negative?"

As Damon continues the process of homosexual recovery, Chris feels many emotional ups and downs. Chris summarizes her current outlook this way: "I know that my precious son is in good hands. My greatest joy is knowing that when we both die, we will be together for eternity. My prayers have been answered. The prodigal son has returned to serve his Father."

Today Damon is working as one of the leaders in New Hope, our local ex-gay outreach in San Rafael, California. He is healthy and doing well with the Lord. We are proud of his accomplishments and thrilled to have his participation in our ministry. His mother continues to rejoice in the good work that God has done in her son's life.

"Homosexuality is not a hopeless condition," she says with conviction. "There is restoration and forgiveness and healing through Jesus Christ. Today, Damon is wise beyond his years. I rejoice to see his growth and also his love for God. Most of all, I'm grateful to our loving Father, the One who lifted both of us from the depths of despair."[5]

The Ongoing Journey

Unlike Chris, most of you are family members and friends who, like me, have a loved one still in rebellion. And like me, you probably vacillate between hope and fear. My fear seems to smolder just below the surface, ready to be sparked into a raging fire.

Last week I was getting ready to attend an important annual event for our ministry, when the men in our live-in program are introduced to our church during a special Sunday-evening service. In the late afternoon I phoned Tony to see how he was doing. "I don't feel well," he said, "and I don't have any food in the house." I checked my watch as I wrote out a short shopping list on the back of an envelope.

Later, while I was shopping, I felt tempted to give in to anger and fear. Anger at God for the timing of Tony's request, and fear that his latest health problems could be serious.

By the time I reached Tony's apartment with the groceries, he was feeling better. "Thanks, Mom!" he said, reaching for the bags I had brought. After paying me for the bill, he said goodby. I stood for a moment looking at the closed door before turning away.

Later, I felt excited and refreshed as I watched our church respond with love and open arms to our program members. But I couldn't help comparing their situation with my son's. Tony was probably asleep in front of a flickering television in his dark, cluttered apartment. At our church, only blocks away, our ministry members were surrounded by a roomful of people radiating love and joy.

Even as I felt a moment of sadness for my son, I had to remember that his situation was the result of *his* ongoing choices. And I also had a choice: I could worry about him, or I could release him once again and enjoy the good things happening around me.

As I glanced back in the auditorium from my seat near the front, I noticed many graduates from past programs who had come to participate in this special evening. Some of them were sitting beside their spouses; all of them were celebrating with us the excitement of what God was doing in our midst. The service was marvelous, with the men providing special instrumental music, a choral selection and several testimonies of their hopes and dreams for the coming years. After the service I hugged two sets of parents who still had children involved in homosexuality, but who had come to support the program members in their quest for new freedom.

I am so glad that I did not give in to my anger and fear at the supermarket earlier that day. Being involved in the lives of other people helps me to fight those negative feelings. I can't feel hopeless while surrounded by men and women whom God is restoring in such a powerful way. And I know that hope is not limited to my son's coming out of homosexuality; I have faith in God's ability to carry me when I cannot stand on my own.

Based on what God has done—and continues to do—in my life, I encourage you to look to him for your hope and strength each day. Then be generous to share with others what he gives you. Fear and discouragement do not have to win. When I cling to Jesus and his love for me, I have peace once again.

Exposing my life so deeply in these pages has brought me a mixture of joy and pain—mostly joy. I hope my honesty will help you find words to express the many emotions that may still be locked inside your heart. Let's both continue our journey, taking it just one step at a time. God promises good days ahead for those who place their hope in him.

13
Afterword

As this book goes to press, my son, Tony, is alive—but growing weaker from the ravages of HIV disease. He has not yet expressed a desire to recommit his life to Christ.

Daily I live with a mixture of joy and pain. I like the illustration used by Corrie ten Boom, who explained that God is using the experiences of our lives to weave a pattern. We see only the knots and tangled threads, as if viewed from behind. Someday when we enter God's presence, we will see the beautiful design on the front that he crafted with exquisite wisdom and skill during our earthly existence.

So until then I press on, every day practicing the lessons of perseverance and relinquishment that I have discussed throughout this book.

I don't know what the future holds, but I know who holds the future. For today, his grace is sufficient.

Anita Worthen
March 1996

Appendix A

For Further Reading

Insights for Parents (General)

Johnson, Barbara. *Where Does a Mother Go to Resign?* Minneapolis: Bethany House, 1979, 1994. The gripping story of one woman's struggle to cope with the crippling of her husband, the deaths of two sons and the homosexuality of a third son who disappeared into the gay lifestyle for more than eleven years.

Mitchell, Marcia. *Surviving the Prodigal Years.* Lynnwood, Wash.: Emerald Books, 1995. One mother's advice on "how to love your wayward child without ruining your own life."

White, John. *Parents in Pain.* Downers Grove, Ill.: InterVarsity Press, 1979. *The* classic book for parents with erring children. Highly recommended.

Facing Sorrow and Depression

Johnson, Barbara. *Stick a Geranium in Your Hat and Be Happy!* Dallas: Word, 1990. The author, whose life has been marked by multiple tragedies, encourages us to look for "life's little sparkles" in the midst of our most crippling sorrows. This humorous book will give you a lift even on the darkest days. By the same author: *Fresh Elastic for Stretched-Out Moms* (Old Tappan, N.J.: Fleming H. Revell, 1986); *Splashes of Joy in the Cesspools of Life* (Dallas: Word, 1992); *Pack Up Your Gloomees in a Great Big Box* (Dallas: Word, 1993); *Mama, Get the Hammer! There's a Fly on Papa's Head!* (Dallas: Word, 1994).

Insights into Homosexuality

Dallas, Joe. *Desires in Conflict.* Eugene, Ore.: Harvest House, 1991. A helpful book on overcoming homosexuality, especially for men. Excellent to give a male loved one who is open to seeking change.

Davies, Bob, and Lori Rentzel. *Coming Out of Homosexuality.* Downers Grove, Ill.: InterVarsity Press, 1993. This book will give you an inside look at the issues faced by the man or woman seeking to overcome homosexuality. Offers practical help for your loved one if he or she is interested in seeking change. An appendix in the back gives answers to common "pro-gay Christian" arguments.

Howard, Jeanette. *Out of Egypt: Leaving Lesbianism Behind.* Eastbourne, U.K.: Monarch, 1991. Excellent insights into overcoming lesbianism. This is a great book to give a female relative who is seeking change. (Available in North America through Regeneration Books, P.O. Box 9830, Baltimore, MD 21284.)

Konrad, Jeff. *You Don't Have to Be Gay.* Hilo, Hawaii: Pacific Publishing, 1987, 1992. A series of letters written by a former homosexual to his unsaved gay friend. This is the best book to give an unsaved homosexual as a witness that homosexuality can be changed. (Available through Regeneration Books, P.O. Box 9830, Baltimore, MD 21284.)

Riley, Mona, and Brad Sargent. *Unwanted Harvest?* Nashville: Broadman and Holman, 1995. A challenge to complacent churches: the harvest fields within the gay community are ripe for harvest, but few are willing to reap.

Worthen, Frank. *Helping People Step Out of Homosexuality.* A practical and encouraging book on overcoming homosexuality, written by one of the founders of the ex-gay movement. (Privately published; available in North America through Regeneration Books, P.O. Box 9830, Baltimore, MD 21284.)

Troubled Marriages

Barshinger, Clark E., Lojan E. LaRowe and Andrés Tapia. *Haunted Marriage.* Downers Grove, Ill.: InterVarsity Press, 1995. Insights for the husband whose wife is dealing with past sexual abuse.

Carter, Les. *The Prodigal Spouse.* Nashville: Thomas Nelson, 1990. A book to help readers sort through the consequences of adultery.

Conway, Jim, and Sally Conway. *Moving On After He Moves Out.* Downers Grove, Ill.: InterVarsity Press, 1995. Sympathetic help for the abandoned wife.

Courtright, John, and Sid Rogers. *Your Wife Was Sexually Abused.* Grand Rapids Mich.: Zondervan, 1994. Two husbands share what they have learned in helping their wives deal with past abuse.

Harley, Willard F., Jr. *His Needs, Her Needs.* Old Tappan, N.J.: Fleming H. Revell, 1986. Excellent for understanding the emotional needs of your spouse or helping your spouse to understand your needs.

Harvey, Donald R. *Surviving Betrayal.* Grand Rapids, Mich.: Baker, 1995. Detailed help for couples whose marriage has been devastated by an affair. Also includes help in facing the marital problems which existed before the betrayal.

Hybels, Bill, and Lynne Hybels. *Fit to Be Tied.* Grand Rapids, Mich.: Zondervan, 1991. Helpful principles interwoven with the interesting story of a pastor and his wife who had numerous incompatibilities to resolve.

Northington, Jan. *Separated and Waiting.* Nashville: Thomas Nelson, 1994. Practical help on "how to find direction and comfort in the midst of marital separation."

Williams, Pat, and Jill Williams, with Jerry Jenkins. *Rekindled.* Old Tappan, N.J.:

Fleming H. Revell, 1985. This is a superb book for the husband who is trying to reestablish emotional intimacy with his wife. Written by a couple whose marriage was emotionally dead, it tells how their relationship was revived.

Healthy Relationships

Beattie, Melodie. *Codependent No More.* New York: HarperCollins, 1987. *The* classic book on codependency (secular).

Ells, Alfred. *One-Way Relationships.* Nashville: Thomas Nelson, 1990. What to do when "you love them more than they love you."

Groom, Nancy. *From Bondage to Bonding.* Colorado Springs, Colo.: NavPress, 1991. A practical, biblical book on overcoming codependency.

Romantic Friendships

Arterburn, Steve. *Addicted to "Love."* Ann Arbor, Mich.: Servant, 1991. Overcoming unhealthy dependencies in romance, relationships and sex.

Rentzel, Lori. *Emotional Dependency.* Downers Grove, Ill.: InterVarsity Press, 1991. Helpful insights when a friendship has become too emotionally enmeshed.

Smith, M. Blaine. *Should I Get Married?* Downers Grove, Ill.: InterVarsity Press, 1990. Crucial reading for making the big decision.

Warren, Neil Clark. *Finding the Love of Your Life.* Colorado Springs, Colo.: Focus on the Family, 1992. Practical advice on one of life's biggest decisions.

Dealing with HIV/AIDS

Allen, Jimmy. *Burden of a Secret.* Nashville: Moorings/Ballantine, 1995. A grandfather and national Baptist leader watches as four members of his extended family battle the onslaught of HIV illness.

Fisher, Kathy, Bob Fisher and Debbie Bennett. *A Mother's Heart, a Father's Hurt, a Sister's Love.* Privately published; available through Regeneration Books, P.O. Box 9830, Baltimore, MD 21284. How one family came to rely on God's help to cope with the homosexuality and HIV disease of a son.

Greif, Judith, and Beth Ann Golden. *AIDS Care at Home: A Guide for Caregivers, Loved Ones and People with AIDS.* New York: John Wiley & Sons, 1994. A guide for caregivers, loved ones and people with AIDS. This book is a complete source of medical, psychological and nutritional information and practical advice for day-to-day living (secular).

Jarvis, Debra. *The Journey Through AIDS: A Guide for Loved Ones and Caregivers.* Batavia, Ill.: Lion, 1992. One of the few religious titles offering practical insights into caring for a loved one with AIDS. It is not evangelical but is an excellent title to share with non-Christian family members and friends.

Perry, Shireen, with Gregg Lewis. *In Sickness and in Health.* Fascinating account of a couple whose marriage is devastated by AIDS, due to the husband's previous homosexual involvement. (Privately published; available through Re-generation Books, P.O. Box 9830, Baltimore, MD 21284.)

Countering the Pro-Gay Theology
Schmidt, Thomas E. *Straight & Narrow?* Downers Grove, Ill.: InterVarsity Press, 1995. An outstanding resource if your loved one embraces the pro-gay theological viewpoint and you want to delve deeply into the Scriptures to defend your traditional moral views on homosexuality.

Countering Gay Militancy/Activism
Magnuson, Roger. *Informed Answers to Gay Rights Questions.* Sisters, Ore.: Multnomah, 1994. A Christian lawyer offers straight answers to the claims and demands of the modern pro-gay movement. This book is recommended if your gay loved one is overwhelming you with gay-rights rhetoric and you want solid answers in terms of the current law and public policy. (This information, for example, might be important for ex-spouses dealing with custody battles.) By the same author: *Are Gay Rights Right?* (Sisters, Ore.: Multnomah, 1990).

Appendix B

Resources for Additional Help

Local Support Groups

Exodus International is a worldwide coalition of Christian ministries that offer support to men and women seeking to overcome homosexuality. Many of these ministries have specialized services for family members and friends, including support groups, one-on-one counseling, literature and other helpful resources. For a free introductory packet of literature on the work of Exodus, including a complete list of referral ministries, contact Exodus International—North America, P.O. Box 77652, Seattle, WA 98177 (206/784-7799).

Overseas readers can contact the appropriate office:

Europe: Exodus International—Europe, P.O. Box 407, Watford WD1 5DU, United Kingdom.

Australia and New Zealand: Exodus International—South Pacific, P.O. Box 308, Fortitude Valley, Queensland 4006, Australia.

Latin America: Exodus International—Latin America, P.O. Box 26202, Colorado Springs, CO 80936, U.S.A.

Singapore: Choices, c/o Church of Our Saviour, 130 Margaret Drive, Singapore 0314.

Philippines: Bagong Pag-asa, P.O. Box 9139, MCS Mailing Center, 1200 Makati, MM, Philippines.

All other overseas locations: Exodus International—North America, P.O. Box 77652, Seattle, WA 98177, U.S.A.

Audiotapes

Each year Exodus International—North America hosts a national conference on overcoming homosexuality. Dozens of workshops are professionally audiotaped, covering many topics of special interest to family members and friends with a gay loved one. For a free catalog, contact Exodus International—North America, P.O. Box 77652, Seattle, WA 98177 (206/784-7799).

Books

Many excellent books can help you deal with your loved one's homosexuality. Ask for titles at your local Christian bookstore. If you prefer, you can conveniently obtain many of these books by mail. For a free catalog of books on homo sexuality and related issues, contact Regeneration Books, P.O. Box 9830, Baltimore, MD 21284 (410/661-0284).

Phone Support
One of the authors, Anita Worthen, is available to offer you support by phone during weekdays (no collect calls, please). You can contact her at New Hope Ministries, P.O. Box 10246, San Rafael, CA 94912 (415/453-6475).

Notes

Chapter 1: Homosexuality: The Shocking Discovery
[1]Portions of this testimony are adapted from Beth Babb, "God Restored My Marriage" (Love In Action, P.O. Box 753307, Memphis, TN 38175). Used by permission.

Chapter 2: The Grief Cycle: Surviving the Emotional Turmoil
[1]Barbara Johnson, *Where Does a Mother Go to Resign?* (Minneapolis: Bethany House, 1979), p. 10.
[2]Grief wheel diagram courtesy of Nurses Christian Fellowship, n.d.
[3]Tom Taylor, "Homosexuality in the Family: A Father's Response," *Harvest News,* Spring 1991, p. 1. Published by Harvest USA, P.O. Box 11469, Philadelphia, PA 19111.
[4]Barbara Johnson, *Stick a Geranium in Your Hat and Be Happy!* (Dallas: Word, 1990), p. 38.
[5]Mary Lebsock, "What I've Learned as a Mother," testimony distributed by Love In Action, P.O. Box 753307, Memphis, TN 38175.
[6]Dwight L. Carlson, *Why Do Christians Shoot Their Wounded?* (Downers Grove, Ill.: InterVarsity Press, 1994), p. 9.
[7]Johnson, *Stick a Geranium,* p. 163.
[8]Ibid., p. 177.

Chapter 3: Guilt: The Continual Crushing Weight
[1]This is true for both gay men and lesbians. See J. M. Bailey and R. C. Pillard, "A Genetic Study of Male Sexual Orientation," *Archives of General Psychiatry* 48 (1991): 1089-96; J. M. Bailey et al., "Heritable Factors Influence Sexual Orientation in Women," *Archives of General Psychiatry* 50 (1993): 217-23.
[2]For a thorough discussion of the psychological literature which supports the idea that homosexuality is not genetic, see Joseph Nicolosi, *Reparative Therapy of Male Homosexuality* (Northvale, N.J.: Jason Aronson, 1991).
[3]We recommend the excellent book *Straight & Narrow?* by Thomas Schmidt (Downers Grove, Ill.: InterVarsity Press, 1995). For a short but thorough summary, see appendix A in the book *Coming Out of Homosexuality* by Bob Davies and Lori Rentzel (Downers Grove, Ill.: InterVarsity Press, 1993).
[4]Corrie ten Boom, *Not Good If Detached* (Fort Washington, Penn.: Christian Literature Crusade, 1957), p. 42.

[5]Corrie ten Boom, *Tramp for the Lord* (Fort Washington, Penn.: Christian Literature Crusade, 1974), p. 183.

Chapter 5: Relinquishment: What Does "Letting Go" Really Mean?
[1]Some portions of this chapter are adapted from the article "Relinquishment: What Does 'Letting Go' Really Mean?" by Lori Rentzel and Bob Davies. Distributed by Love In Action, P.O. Box 753307, Memphis, TN 38175. Used by permission.
[2]Barbara Johnson, *Where Does a Mother Go to Resign?* (Minneapolis: Bethany House, 1979, 1994), pp. 116-17.
[3]This section is adapted from "Letting Go of Love" by DebbieLynne Simmons, an article distributed by Love In Action, P.O. Box 753307, Memphis, TN 38175. Some quotes are taken from "Answering God's Call" by DebbieLynne Simmons (Love In Action, 1992). All material is used by permission.

Chapter 6: Sexual Abuse: Uncovering Another Family Secret
[1]Jan Frank, *A Door of Hope* (Nashville: Thomas Nelson, 1995), pp. 65-67.
[2]Ibid., p. 100.
[3]Clark E. Barshinger, Lojan E. LaRowe and Andrés Tapia, *Haunted Marriage* (Downers Grove, Ill.: InterVarsity Press, 1995), p. 9. The remainder of this anecdote is adapted from the prologue (pp. 9-16).
[4]Don Frank and Jan Frank, *When Victims Marry* (Nashville: Thomas Nelson, 1990), p. 90.
[5]Kay Scott, *Sexual Assault* (Minneapolis: Bethany House, 1993), p. 132.
[6]Alfred Ells, *Restoring Innocence* (Nashville: Thomas Nelson, 1990), p. 190. Some material in this section is adapted from pp. 190-92. Used by permission.
[7]Scott, *Sexual Assault*, p. 135.
[8]Adapted from Ells, *Restoring Innocence,* pp. 190-92. Used by permission.
[9]Frank, *When Victims Marry,* p. 159. Other material in this section is adapted from the same page. Used by permission.
[10]Ibid., p. 153.
[11]Barshinger, LaRowe and Tapia, *Haunted Marriage,* pp. 108, 114.
[12]Ibid., p. 208.

Chapter 7: Illness: Living in the Shadow of AIDS
[1]Excellent titles include *The Essential HIV Treatment Fact Book* by Laura Pinsky and Paul Harding Douglas with Craig Metroka (New York: Pocket Books, 1992); *AIDS Care at Home: A Guide for Caregivers, Loved Ones and People with AIDS* by Judith Grief and Beth Anne Golden (New York: John Wiley and Sons, 1994);

214 SOMEONE I LOVE IS GAY

214 ■ SOMEONE I LOVE IS GAY

and *Guide to Living with HIV Infection* by John G. Bartlett and Ann K. Finkbeiner (Baltimore: Johns Hopkins University Press, 1993). Your local bookstore may be able to assist you in finding similar but more current titles.
[2]Charles F. Stanley, "Passion for God" tape series (available through In Touch Ministries, P.O. Box 7900, Atlanta, GA 30357).
[3]Henri J. M. Nouwen, *Who We Are* (New York: Crossroad, 1994), pp. 139-40.
[4]Bob Winter as told to Bob Davies, "A Gift Beyond Measure," *The Lookout*, February 4, 1990, p. 9.

Chapter 8: Just for Parents: Special Concerns & Questions
[1]Lori Rentzel, *Emotional Dependency* (Downers Grove, Ill.: InterVarsity Press, 1990). Material in this section is adapted from pp. 8-9.
[2]Adapted from Tom Taylor, "Homosexuality in the Family: A Father's Response," *Harvest News*, Spring 1991 (Harvest USA, P.O. Box 11469, Philadelphia, PA 19111).
[3]Jeanette Howard, *Out of Egypt: Leaving Lesbianism Behind* (Eastbourne, E. Sussex, U.K.: Monarch, 1991), p. 77.
[4]Adapted from "Uncovering the Real Me" by Starla Allen as told to Bob Davies (Love In Action, P.O. Box 753307, Memphis, TN 38175).
[5]Dorothy Allan, "God Is Faithful!" (Love In Action, P.O. Box 753307, Memphis, TN 38175).

Chapter 9: Just for Spouses: Special Concerns & Questions
[1]Adapted from Sheila Jean Hood, *Double Life* (Wheaton, Ill.: Tyndale, 1991), pp. 45-46. Used by permission.
[2]For excellent insights into this situation, we highly recommend the booklet by Lori Rentzel, *Emotional Dependency* (Downers Grove, Ill.: InterVarsity Press, 1990).
[3]Taken from the audiotape "Lesbianism and the Married Woman" by Carol Fryer (Exodus International, 1992).
[4]Taken from the audiotape "Straight Husbands of Ex-Gay Women" by Douglas Geyer and Stan Harris (Exodus International, 1993).
[5]See Barbara Dafoe Whitehead, "Dan Quayle Was Right," *Atlantic Monthly*, April 1993, p. 47.
[6]Jim Talley, personal interview with the authors. Dr. Talley is owner/counselor at Relationship Resources in Oklahoma City (800/645-3761).
[7]See the multitude of examples in Bob Davies and Lori Rentzel, *Coming Out of Homosexuality* (Downers Grove, Ill.: InterVarsity Press, 1993).
[8]This section is adapted from "The Valley of Trouble, the Door of Hope" by Robbi Kenney (Metanoia Ministries newsletter, P.O. Box 33039, Seattle, WA

98133), March and April 1984. Used by permission.

[9]Jim Conway and Sally Conway, *Moving On After He Moves Out* (Downers Grove, Ill.: InterVarsity Press, 1995), p. 102.

[10]Hood, *Double Life*, p. 86.

[11]Portions of this anecdote are taken from the audiotape "Help! My Husband Is Gay" by Willa Medinger (Exodus International, 1990). The remainder is taken from personal interviews by the authors.

[12]For a man's perspective on saving an emotionally deprived marriage, pick up a copy of the outstanding paperback *Rekindled* by Pat and Jill Williams with Jerry Jenkins (Old Tappan, N.J.: Fleming H. Revell, 1985). Other books are mentioned in appendix A.

[13]Adapted from Lisa Stricker, "Out of Fear, Grief and Anger," *Exodus Update* (Exodus International), October 1995.

Chapter 10: When a Friend Says, "I'm Gay"

[1]Williams H. Masters and Virginia E. Johnson, *Homosexuality in Perspective* (Boston: Little, Brown and Company, 1979), p. 182.

[2]Taken from "Condemn the Sin, Not the Sinner," posted in the *Christianity Today* section of America Online, August 1995.

[3]Adapted from "Taking Off the Mask" by John Paulk, a testimony distributed by Love In Action, P.O. Box 753307, Memphis, TN 38175. Used by permission.

[4]Many ideas in this section are adapted from Lori Rentzel, "My Friend Is Struggling with Homosexuality" (Love In Action, P.O. Box 753307, Memphis, TN 38175). Used by permission.

Chapter 12: Finding Hope Again: Life After Homosexuality

[1]Corrie ten Boom, *Don't Wrestle, Just Nestle* (Old Tappan, N.J.: Fleming H. Revell, 1978), pp. 42, 58.

[2]Barbara Johnson, *Mama, Get the Hammer! There's a Fly on Papa's Head!* (Dallas: Word, 1994), p. 45.

[3]To contact Barbara, write to Spatula Ministries, P.O. Box 444, La Habra, CA 90633.

[4]Barbara Johnson, *Pack Up Your Gloomees in a Great Big Box* (Dallas: Word, 1993), pp. 59, 117, 141.

[5]Adapted from Chris MacKenzie, "Help—My Son Is Gay!" (Love In Action, P.O. Box 753307, Memphis, TN 38175). Used by permission.

About the Authors

Anita Worthen has been involved with ex-gay ministry to family members and friends for over twelve years. She and her husband, Frank, one of the founders of the ex-gay movement, have spoken about homosexual ministry on four continents. They work together at New Hope Ministries in San Rafael, California. Bob Davies is executive director of Exodus International—North America, a network of agencies for men and women seeking freedom from homosexuality, and is coauthor of *Coming Out of Homosexuality*. He and his wife, Pam, live in Seattle, Washington.

Bob and Anita are available for speaking engagements. You can contact Bob at Exodus International, P.O. Box 77652, Seattle, WA 98177, and Anita at New Hope Ministries, P.O. Box 10246, San Rafael, CA 94912.